# DISCOURSE
# AND COMMUNITY

## MULTIDISCIPLINARY STUDIES
## OF CANADIAN CULTURE

Essay Series 53

Canada Council   Conseil des Arts
for the Arts      du Canada

ONTARIO ARTS COUNCIL
CONSEIL DES ARTS DE L'ONTARIO

Guernica Editions Inc. acknowledges the support
of The Canada Council for the Arts.
Guernica Editions Inc. acknowledges the support
of the Ontario Arts Council.

# DISCOURSE

# AND COMMUNITY

## MULTIDISCIPLINARY STUDIES
## OF CANADIAN CULTURE

### EDITED BY HOWARD A. DOUGHTY
### AND MARINO TUZI

## GUERNICA

TORONTO – BUFFALO – CHICAGO – LANCASTER (U.K.)
2007

Howard A. Doughty and Marino Tuzi, Guest Editors
Guernica Editions Inc.
P.O. Box 117, Station P, Toronto (ON), Canada M5S 2S6
2250 Military Road, Tonawanda, N.Y. 14150-6000 U.S.A.


Distributors:
University of Toronto Press Distribution,
5201 Dufferin Street, Toronto, (ON), Canada M3H 5T8
Gazelle Book Services, White Cross Mills, High Town,
Lancaster LA1 4XS U.K.
Independent Publishers Group,
814 N. Franklin Street, Chicago, Il. 60610 U.S.A.


Typeset by Selina.
Printed in Canada.
First edition.


Legal Deposit — First Quarter
National Library of Canada
Library of Congress Catalog Card Number: 2006929306
Library and Archives Canada Cataloguing in Publication
Discourse and community :
multidisciplinary studies of Canadian culture /
edited by Howard A. Doughty and Marino Tuzi.
(Essay series ; 53)
ISBN 1-55071-256-X
1. Canada–Civilization.
I. Doughty, Howard A., 1945- II. Tuzi, Marino, 1952-
III. Series: Essay series (Toronto, Ont.)
FC95.5.D48 2006      971      C2006-903618-7

# Contents

This book is dedicated to the memory of Frank Eastham (1944-1998) and of Kay Eastham (1946-2002), each of whom lived well and differently, and both of whom were friends who died too young. "Larger than life," Frank gave tirelessly to Canada's trade union movement and the education of workers. Kay was a selfless public servant who dedicated her life to the successful advocacy of equity and social justice. They are missed, but their legacies are an invaluable part of our heritage. So this book is also dedicated to the future of Emma Eastham and to Canadians of her generation, who have a lifetime to grow and enjoy.

# Preface

## Marino Tuzi

The essays in this book focus on a variety of topics and issues from within the parameters of specific and established fields of study. Some of the essays examine ideas and events pertaining to time periods in the past, while other essays probe the significance of contemporary social and cultural reality. In all these essays, particular aspects of Canadian society are investigated, revealing not just the merit of what is being specifically investigated, but also, either directly or indirectly, emphasizing the value of analyzing the many elements that constitute Canadian society.

If there is any kind of common ground shared by the writers of the various essays, it exists in the fact that they seem committed to the underlying idea that the act of observing and analyzing makes one conscious of the dimensions of one's culture and society. The meaning of a particular element of a national culture is not necessarily intrinsic or self-evident. Instead, it is through a process of investigation that essayists locate the many meanings of specific events or activities. Equally important, the essayists invest meaning into what is being examined from the perspective of their academic or philosophical orientations.

As such, this book of essays provides a multidisciplinary view of the different facets of Canadian culture and society. Although the titles of the essays in the table of contents are grouped under two major categories, literary and cultural studies and social and political studies, the intent of this organization is not to delineate sharp disciplinary boundaries among the essays. Instead, the organization of the contents is meant to facilitate the reader's understanding of the scope and nature of the contributions, and, at the same time, to emphasize the various sensibilities that have been brought to the study of the many aspects of Canadian culture and society. Furthermore, in some of the essays, the writers have deployed tools of analysis from several disciplines, such as sociology, political economy, and cultural anthropology, or such as literary criticism and cultural studies. This approach serves to reinforce the multifarious critical orientation of the book. The study of Canadian culture and society is ultimately inclusive, since what is significant is not solely the particular area that is under scrutiny. In examining the cultural components of a given society, critical thinkers not only highlight the complex textures and the startling contradictions of that society. Critical thinkers also affirm the importance, ethically and politically, of making a specific society and its diverse elements knowable to its people and to the rest of the world.

In closing, Howard Doughty and I would like to acknowledge the support and guidance that we received from Antonio D'Alfonso, the publisher and senior editor of Guernica Editions, in bringing this endeavour to fruition.

# Foreword

## Howard A. Doughty

Three-quarters of a century ago, England's G. K. Chesterton, the witty, versatile, romantic medievalist and anti-socialist polemicist, was strongly praised in an early essay by Canada's Marshall McLuhan. In Chesterton's view (which McLuhan faithfully presents and which I cheerfully cleave from its context), "the cynical social legislation of today, undertaken in supposed accord with unyielding economic circumstances, is often light-headed because it is not light-hearted."[1] The words do not seem out of place today.

Marshall McLuhan was an exemplary Canadian intellectual of the 1930s. Studying in England prior to teaching in Wisconsin, he brushed, however briefly, against this country's imperial touchstones. Fellow Canadian and future economist Tom Easterbrook introduced McLuhan to Chesterton's *What's Wrong with the World* while they were doctoral students at Cambridge. Not long afterwards, McLuhan (like Chesterton before him) became what he was often pleased to call "the worst kind of Catholic, a convert." Fondness for Chesterton is easily acquired by reading McLuhan's then-fresh disquisition:

> Chesterton is the champion of the English poor. He is the mouthpiece of the poor who cannot hear him. He is their memory and their poet, the cherisher of their traditions stamped out by misery, and the singer of virtues they have almost forgotten. And his sympathies are a proof of his splendid lineage.[2]

Chesterton's poetry is cited:

> I saw great Cobbett riding,
> The horseman of the shires;
> And his face was red with judgment
> And a light of Luddite fires.[3]

Chesterton's prose is quoted:

> Cobbett was defeated because the English people was defeated. After the frame-breaking riots, men as men were beaten. And Ireland did not get home rule because England didn't.[4]

What English Canadian of his era, who chose or was chosen to be exempt from loyalty to the colonial establishment, could fail to love such a man as McLuhan thus portrays him?[5] Chesterton, according to McLuhan, was "a revolutionary, not because he finds everything equally detestable, but because he fears lest certain infinitely valuable things should vanish."[6] Many of these valuable things were inconsistent with Whiggery, the emerging ideology of industrial capitalism.[7]

In Canada, too, the nineteenth-century colonial establishment had sometimes displayed an ambivalent attitude toward the new world order of the day. James George, the Acting Principal of Queen's University, for example, was a champion of organized religion, a monarchist and an imperialist who disdained democracy. Paternalistic in all matters of political relations, he replied to the rebellions of 1837 and 1838 with an uncompromising sermon "On the Duties of Subjects to Their Rulers." Yet, he made this declaration:

> The factory system in England has been the means of acquiring great wealth for individuals as well as for the country, yet, who is so ignorant as not to know that, as it has generally been carried on, it has tended to reduce masses of the working classes physically, as well as mentally, to great degradation. The accumulation of wealth, then, among a people – especially when accumulated in a few hands – is not necessarily a civi-

lizing agency, and in fact, may be a great enemy to true civilization.[8]

Such exhibitions of nascent "Red Toryism" stand markedly apart from the sentiments of those who call themselves "conservatives" today. Still, it was not so long ago that the Conservative Party in Canada "held to policies not far from their 'socialist' rivals." Public enterprise in transportation, communications, electricity generation and many other fields was, for example, preferred to private ownership by numerous Conservative federal and provincial governments. So, intellectual historians Leslie Armour and Elizabeth Trott explain that "hardly anyone was surprised" when a philosopher like George Grant moved easily between the Conservative and the New Democratic parties, seeing in both a similar commitment to the community over unfettered individual rights. Both tories and social democrats, after all, "preached social responsibility, the containment of the most virulent kinds of individualism, orderly social change."[9] Precisely this apparent convergence in conservative and radical thought has been discussed by many students of the Canadian polity. It was, however, most compellingly appraised and identified as a singular, perhaps even a defining, aspect of Canadian political thought by Gad Horowitz. In an influential argument first presented in 1966, he credited the presence of tory ideology with making possible the development of an influential socialist ideology and praised both for ensuring "the legitimacy of ideological diversity in English Canada."[10]

For some, Red Toryism and democratic socialism have both been eclipsed by the dominant neoliberal ideas that serve to sustain capitalist globalization. Moreover, while many contemporary nationalistic, postcolonial, and multicultural Canadian readers find McLuhan remote enough, they regard G.K. Chesterton merely as an imperial atavism relevant only to those who warmly recall the Union Jack unfurled on "Dominion Day." Most have never heard of James George and are too quickly forgetting George Grant. Still, there is a point to mentioning them all. If only as reminders of antique imperial days, theirs are legitimate voices – now historical – that once influenced indirectly or directly important elements of Canadian society and culture.[11] They detested some things and valued others.

Each essay in this book in some way alludes to what is detestable and to what is valuable, to what may be in danger of vanishing. Some of the detestable things are cravenness, churlishness and meanness; some of the valuable things are courage, civility and good humour. The former are evident in the intolerance, greed and repression seen around us. The latter are related to the good society we have yet to build but intimations of which are manifest in our historical traditions and in the best of our contemporary ideas and actions. As such, we have no shortage of certified visionaries, pundits and spin doctors who are eager to show us how poverty, bigotry and alienation can and will be ameliorated or even eliminated through an uncritical embrace of the economics, politics and technology of the twenty-first century. In this newly dubbed "postmodern" society, we are oxymoronically invited to submit to the dictates of an electronic "global village" headed by transnational corporate chieftains, while simultaneously celebrating diversity and our own unique cultural "industries." We are urged to strive for competitive excellence and let Canadian cultural "products" find their value in the world market.[12]

. Upon hearing such light-headed talk, we may be forgiven if we sometimes empathize with McLuhan's affirmation: "I have never been an optimist or a pessimist. I'm an apocalyptic only. Our only hope is apocalypse."[13] So bring on the horsemen! Or, maybe there is something less dramatic and more democratic to be done. Perhaps, we can draw attention to the pernicious sores on our body politic, and devise ways in which some of them may be arithmetically reduced and others may eventually be healed. From our history, we can recover tokens of virtue. We can sense, in our present, glimmers of hope and give new energy to the Canadian polity.

As Charles Taylor, one of our finest contemporary philosophers, reminds us, Canadian "liberals have long since squandered all their moral capital: their philosophy was bankrupt." Conservatives, on the other hand, at least recalled when their beliefs meant something. So "the dying [Donald] Creighton lashed out with anguished fury at all those who had betrayed Macdonald's vision." So, too, Taylor went on, "the great organ voice of George Grant boomed out an awesome threnody, not only for a distinctive Canada, but also for almost any concept of human diversity and individual excellence." Young people today should understand their lamentations, he said, as "not so much an excuse for despair as a bracing challenge to rectify the mistakes of their elders." Thus, Taylor concluded, their noble and genuinely compassionate conservatism (as distinct from George W. Bush's unctuous Whiggish bromide), "provided the basis for something greater than the imperative of Sir Thomas More: 'When you can't make good things happen, try to prevent the very worst.' "[14]

The writings collected herein may yield no formula for recovery from the disillusionment of a progressive modernity that unraveled in the monstrous horrors of the twentieth century, nor the anxiety that is to be experienced in the twenty-first, as an amoral postmodernity carries on, sustained by technology out of control. They do, however, speak of things we must criticize and things we may praise. In at least one case, there is a modest display of self-mockery, undertaken with the dual convictions that light-hearted need not necessarily mean light-headed, and that critical thinking could certainly stand a little playfulness.

In any case, whether in politics or in art, it is neither too late to find the will to resist detestable things nor the means to contribute to the store of valuable things. To do so, we need only speak to one another in the interest of what we share.

## Notes

1. Marshall McLuhan, "G. K. Chesterton: A Practical Mystic," *Dalhousie Review* (January, 1936), reprinted in Eric McLuhan and Jacek Szklarek, eds., *The Medium and the Light: Reflections on Religion* (Toronto: Stoddart, 1999), p. 3.

2. *Ibid.*, p. 8.

3. *Ibid.*

4. *Ibid.*

5. Paul Johnson reminds us that William Cobbett, of course, "called himself a Tory." See *The Birth of the Modern: World Society 1815-1830* (New York: HarperCollins, 1991), p. 366. An entertaining account of Cobbett in America is to be found in wordsmith and one time Spiro Agnew speechwriter William Safire's *Scandalmonger* (New York: Simon and Schuster, 2000) a fictional remake, of Gore Vidal's fictional *Burr* (New York: Random House, 1973).

6. McLuhan and Szklarek, *op. cit.*, p. 3. Marshall McLuhan's son, Eric, takes considerable umbrage at the efforts of contemporary media analysts such as Neil Postman and Arthur Kroker to tame McLuhan's religious convictions and discount them as "basically age-old Christian Humanism in modern dress." *Ibid.*, "Introduction," p. xix. His umbrage is, perhaps, well taken.

7. Writes Charles Taylor: "As Northrop Frye has pointed out, since Canadians fought their wars of independence against the United States, it is logical that we should feel a strong suspicion of the mercantilist Whiggery which won the American Revolution (and which, in turn, evolved into the contemporary forces of liberal technology)." *Radical Tories: The Conservative Tradition in Canada* (Toronto: Anansi, 1982), p. 212.

8. Quoted in Leslie Armour and Elizabeth Trott, *The Faces of Reason: An Essay on Philosophy and Culture in English Canada 1850-1950* (Waterloo: Sir Wilfrid Laurier University Press, 1981), p. 46.

9. *Ibid.*, p. 25.

10. Gad Horowitz, "Conservatism, Liberalism and Socialism in Canada: An Interpretation," *The Canadian Journal of Economics and Political Science*, Vol. 32, No. 2 (May, 1966), p. 150, reproduced as

Chapter 1 of *Canadian Labour in Politics* (Toronto: University of Toronto Press, 1968).

11. The heritage of "English" Canada may not be of exclusively antiquarian interest. "The notion of Canadian citizen as opposed to British subject is a very recent one in Canada," explain Armour and Trott (*op. cit.*, p. xxiii). It is a fact to which I can attest having been born in Toronto prior to the passage of the *Canadian Citizenship Act* which won royal assent in 1946, just in time to catch the "baby boomers" in its national net.

12. As Eric McLuhan laconically relates, "for a few years now, the business of business has been culture." *Electric Language: Understanding the Present* (Toronto: Stoddart, 1998), p. 54.

13. Marshall McLuhan, "Futurechurch: Edward Watkin Interviews Marshall McLuhan," *U.S. Catholic*, Vol. 42, No. 1 (January), reprinted *ibid.*, p. 59.

14. Charles Taylor, *op. cit.*, p. 212.

# Literary and Cultural Studies

# Canada's Floral Godmother

## The Subjectivity of Catharine Paar Traill

## Susan Ellis

Catharine Paar Traill, an inexperienced British settler in the bush-country of Upper Canada in the mid-nineteenth century, wrote *The Female Emigrant's Guide* to advise and instruct potential immigrant women of the upper classes, and in doing so, assumed the role of educator and of namer.[1] In purposefully reconstructing the New World socially through language, Traill reinvents the categories of gender and class. As an English gentlewoman by birth and training confronting the moment of first contact with an uncleared and inaccessible old growth forest homestead, Traill found herself in what Judith Butler has termed gender trouble, as the socially understood gender boundaries of nineteenth-century English culture could not be maintained. But she was also in class trouble: it was impossible to maintain then-current expectations of her proper social role as a lady while performing the heavy manual labour formerly reserved for the working classes. Traill avoids the scandal that the pioneer woman risks of being both unsexed and shamed by loss of class while tilling fields, chopping wood, planting orchards, or clearing brush by signaling not that she is capable, physically strong, or ambitious to invade the territory of masculinity, but merely that she is fulfilling her "natural" domestic femininity by providing services for the benefit of her family. But she expands this domestic domain to include ever-increasing territorial rings moving incrementally outward from the house to the porch, yard, garden, fields, and eventually to the forest itself when Traill takes on the transgressive tasks of naming, cataloging, and documenting the uses of local plant life as she becomes "floral godmother" to Canada. Despite her feminine protestations, Traill's domestic model does pose a delicate form of threat to the masculine realm.

Traill's descriptions of pioneer life are often taken at face value as a "simple, factual, and optimistic account" of her encounters with the Canadian backwoods, as Clara Thomas describes her work in the "Introduction" to *The Canadian Settler's Guide*. Taken as such, Traill's portrayals of settler life are seen as a simple and direct reproduction of pioneer life,[2] "close to the raw stuff of experience."[3] Traill arrived from England in 1832 as a new bride accompanying her husband, a half-pay officer in the Royal Scots Fusiliers, and settled with him on an uncleared military land grant in the vicinity of Peterborough. Her experiences as a female immigrant and settler formed the material for an impressive publishing career, directly in *The Backwoods of Canada* and *The Female Emigrant's Guide*, but also in nature essays and botanical studies, and as background and setting in numerous stories and sketches published both in Great Britain and in Canada.

The cool rationalism and impossible cheerfulness of her writing style are taken so literally by T. D. MacLulich that he mistakenly concluded that she "lives happily ever after" in the Canadian wilds while her less cheerful sister, Susanna Moodie, remained discontented.[4] In fact the Traills failed as settlers, leaving the backwoods in 1839 for village life, possibly because her husband Thomas suffered from depression and despondency in the backwoods.[5] Her writing is sometimes so unproblematically read as simple representations of truth that she has been accused of an unhealthy repression of an assumed universal terror of the wilderness.[6] She seems to "simply walk past – or through – the dragons which beset others [who wrote about the Canadian wilderness such as her sister, Susanna Moodie or Anna Jameson] to look at, then to study, then to describe and classify, the life, especially the plant life, of the world around her."[7]

The fictional character, Morag, in Margaret Laurence's novel *The Diviners*, captures this criticism best when she refers to Traill as Saint Catharine or St. C., in her unbearable practical efficiency, "drawing and naming wild flowers, writing a guide for settlers with one hand, whilst rearing a brace of young and working like a galley slave with the other."[8] Morag conjures up the image of Traill from *The Canadian Settler's Guide* as the epitome of cool efficiency, the antithesis of her own feelings of helpless inadequacy. But in Laurence's novel, Morag is not fooled: she knows that the persona Traill portrays in her pioneer writing is just "too good to be true,"[9] as Morag describes her:

> out of bed, fully awake, bare feet on the sliver-hazardous floor-boards – no, take that one again. Feet on the homemade hooked rug. Breakfast cooked for the multitude. Out to feed the chickens, stopping briefly on the way back to pull fourteen armloads of weeds out of the vegetable garden and perhaps prune the odd apple tree in passing. The children's education hour, the umpteen little mites lisping enthusiastically over this enlightenment. Cleaning the house, baking two hundred loaves of delicious bread, preserving half a ton of plums, pears, cherries, etcetera. All before lunch.[10]

Laurence recognizes the cracks in Traill's portrait; Morag tells the apparition of St. C.: "I suspect you had problems you never let on about."[11] Morag remembers Traill's famous advice from *The Canadian Settler's Guide*: "In cases of emergency, it is folly to fold one's hands and sit down to bewail in abject terror: it is better to be up and doing."[12] Coming as it does in the context of the entire family's battle to save their house from forest fires coming on them from all direc-

tions, Traill's activist stance and her advocacy of optimism as
a deliberate choice should be seen less as a denial of overwhelming danger than as accommodation of its reality. Traill's
writing is laced through with frequent allusions to the terrible trials that await women settlers and to the persistent sor-
row of homesickness that is an intrinsic part of life in the
bush. "Having myself suffered" is the persistent refrain that
characterizes Traill's work, rather than an *absence* of any sign
of the pioneer's anxiety as some critics claim.

Other writers have interpreted her struggle to overcome
such fears as a defining act of liberation, "a sign of their ela-
tion in escaping the confines of social and class strictures of
England, and their new-found freedom and self-sufficien-
cy,"[13] or as a Biblically-inspired story of exile and the founding of a new home which draws its energy from the raw stuff
of the forest.[14] But Traill's persona of the coolly efficient
rationalist is neither the simple reporting of pioneer life, nor
a neurotic repression of normal emotions, nor an emancipa-
tory strategy. She is an ideal, Traill's revised concept of perfect feminine subjectivity that she re-writes in response to
the new circumstances of her life. Traill articulates her own
negotiations with the physical, geographical and social environment of the homesteading pioneer woman in the
Canadian wilderness of the nineteenth century. Those negotiations are gender- and class-specific, as well as being particularly linked to her historical and geographic location. Traill's
writing displays a strong tendency to vindicate Northrop
Frye's assertion that the Canadian sensibility has been formed
by answering, not the question, "Who am I?" but rather the
question, "Where am I?" Traill's answers to this question
write her *place* (both in history and geography) into existence. Traill explicates nineteenth-century Canada to her
readers.[15] But in so doing, she simultaneously writes her *self*,
as well, into existence. Traill's rhetoric of self-disclosure and
factual truth is deceptive; she is consciously and seriously

engaged in reconstructing femininity and selfhood in her new surroundings, by didactically instructing women how socially, sexually, and epistemologically to negotiate the new terrain. She reinvents her place in culture in terms of both gender and class, and her project requires some fancy foot-work.

Some of this negotiation is apparent in Traill's fascination with stories of the child lost in the forest, and the eventual recovery of the child to civilization.[16] Traill not only incorporated this theme into several of her stories and sketches, but her letters and journal entries reveal that she also collected such stories. One of these finds its way into her botanical study of wild plants, *Studies of Plant Life in Canada*, as Traill relates the story of a little girl lost in the bush near Port Hope while picking berries under her botanical description of the swamp blueberry.[17] The lost child/found child tale also forms the basic plot of Traill's novel, *The Canadian Crusoes*, in which three children become lost in the forest searching for cows.[18] Traill's lost child obsession might easily be seen in our post-Freudian era as a recurring waking fantasy with functions similar to those of dream symbolism. The image of the child lost in the woods manifests in story form Traill's psychological grappling with the early settler's fears of being overwhelmed by the unfamiliar, possibly dangerous chaotic presented by the wilderness at their doorstep. If that is so, the lost child/found child ritual that Traill performs over and over again begins to look like Freud's famous "fort-da" game that he observed being played by his eighteen-month-old grandson. The child was extraordinarily well behaved and never cried when his mother left him, but persistently played a game with any object at hand, throwing it away while saying "o-o-o-o," a sound Freud interpreted as the German word "fort" ("gone"). Freud observed the child repeatedly throwing a wooden reel over the edge of his curtained cot to make it disappear, and saying "o-o-o-o", and then pulling the reel back into view with its attached string, and saying with great satisfaction the German word "da" ("there"). Freud concluded that the child was deliberately reenacting the anxiety of his mother's departure and her joyful return in order to master the experience.[19]

William Gairdner comments that the pioneers set about the task of dealing with the fearsome and uncomfortable threat posed by virgin wilderness in a straightforward way: they chopped it down. Traill similarly undertakes the project of making order out of chaos with her pen. She writes the forest into comprehensible pieces, concentrating on naming, cataloguing, and finding useful purposes for the wild plants, trees, and shrubs she encounters. Gaile McGregor diminishes Traill's attempts to cut the forest down to size with sewing scissors,[20] but by bringing the forest under her pen (and also into her garden and cooking pots and onto her table) she comes to terms with an environment she was unprepared for. She also enters the new culture being formed in response to it. When she takes up the pen to describe and instruct, Traill takes on the role of educator and the role of namer. While cloaked in the language of domesticity, Traill's writing gives voice purposefully to the social construction of the new world through language, and a reconstruction of the rules of feminine subjectivity that combines a strategy of resistance to victimization with a rejection of liberationist ideology. While she writes in praise of freedom from the old social constraints and advocates active agency as essential for survival in the new physical and cultural milieu, Traill finds it necessary to re-inscribe the categories of gender and class. Her anxiety to remain a lady despite the necessity of performing the kinds of work formerly assigned to men and to working class women guides her pen.

For when Traill, an English gentlewoman by birth and training, confronts the moment of first contact with the strange new environment of an uncleared and inaccessible homestead in the midst of the old growth Canadian forest, formerly stable notions of what it means to be a woman become unfixed. In order for Traill, as a pioneer woman, to survive in her new wilderness environment, the socially understood boundaries of gender, which she and others brought with them from nineteenth-century English culture cannot be maintained. It is similarly impossible for Traill to maintain the then-current expectations of her proper social role as an upper middle-class gentlewoman as she and her husband eke out a living from the forest. It became imperative to devise new strategies of cultural representation that revised the ways in which her social and political identity could be understood. How does she negotiate, not just the physical wilderness, but the class and gender wilderness of the British pioneer gentlewoman? She does not fold her hands and sit down to bewail in abject terror; she gets up and doing. Her words from *The Settler's Guide*, "Let us now see what can be done" are her motto.[21] Traill's approach to the problem is to seize agency, and to use it simultaneously to subvert and conform to the prevailing class and gender standards. Her "simple, factual" accounts of life in the backwoods disguise within them the working out of a crisis, or scandal, of selfhood and self-definition. Frye's question, "Where am I?" becomes transformed into the autobiographical "I was there," with the corresponding necessity to define both "there" and "I."

Nancy Armstrong provides a useful historical context for examining Traill's crisis of subjectivity. In her analysis, the rise of the figure of the domestic woman in eighteenth-century British culture is a phenomenon that she calls "a major event in political history" because this new kind of woman changed the criteria for determining what was most important in a woman.[22] As a new idea, the figure of the domestic woman gradually replaced the aristocratic cultural ideals of femininity as largely decorative and class as entirely inherited with a class-blind definition of the ideal female in which "neither birth nor the accoutrements of title and status accurately represented the individual; only the subtle nuances of behavior indicated what one was really worth."[23] According to Armstrong, this cultural shift attached moral values to various qualities of the mind, and thus the crucial difference that is gender came to be defined in terms of respective sets of internal qualities that were, in turn, represented as commonsensical.[24] Further, the change in gender criteria to ones that focus on internal qualities meant that all women, regardless of class, could aspire to become the domestic ideal of womanhood, and that life with such a woman was available to all men. Therefore, Armstrong's central argument is that the new ideal served as a cohesive force, creating a common cultural and social interest that excluded only the very powerful aristocrats and the very poor. Thus a social milieu was created that could accommodate the later rise of the middle class in England.[25]

Armstrong provides the historical context of British culture and the domestic woman ideal that shapes Traill's reliance on the internal qualities of mind and spirit she deploys to define and regulate the appropriate form of selfhood for the successful pioneer woman. Traill repeatedly reiterates that it is not in external conditions such as the types of work she must perform or her manner of dress that the pioneer woman must find her self-definition. Rather, it is in her mental attitudes and her cheerful and utilitarian demeanor that her true subjectivity lies. In *The Canadian Settler's Guide*, she begins her advice on preparations for pioneer life with instructions to this effect, warning those contemplating emigration as Canadian settlers that "cheerfulness of mind and activity of body" are essential, and that "persevering energy and industry, with sobriety" will overcome the difficulties of external circumstances.[26] Her message is that, for potential emigrants, the elements of success lie within. Traill advises that newcomers will find it a blessing that external appearance "will not determine social standing or respectability in the colony."[27] Traill assures her readers that, with the proper internal qualities of mind firmly in place, "a lady will be a lady, even in the plainest dress; a vulgar-minded woman will never be a lady, even in the most costly garments."[28] In addition, no amount of money can compensate for the absence of the right sort of mental qualities: optimism, industriousness, and sobriety.

Traill is acutely attentive to anxiety over the necessity for the pioneer woman to perform the labour of men, because to enter the domain of men's labour transgressed common-sensical ideas of the time about what was "natural" for the engendered self. It was essential for the family's survival that a great deal of physical work be performed, but Traill is aware that the pioneer woman risks being unsexed in her own mind and in the minds of her relatives who remain in Britain if she is known to be clearing brush, pulling stumps from the field, tilling with a mule or pulling the plow herself, or planting orchards. Traill avoids the sexual and class scandal brought about by the necessity for ladies not simply to work alongside men but to perform the types of heavy labour formerly reserved in the British culture of the period for working class men and women. Her method in doing so is to appeal to the domestic woman's virtues of utilitarianism, industriousness, and modest self-effacement.

In Traill's characterization of life in the wilderness, the pioneer woman tills the fields not in order to signal that she is capable, physically strong, or ambitious to invade the territory of masculinity, but merely to fulfill her natural domestic femininity by providing a comfortable, charming, and healthful home for the benefit of her family. Even efforts at adornment of the home or its surrounds are advised only because to do so will provide a spiritual benefit for the family, and her love of home extend, in the colonies, woman's "natural" sphere of dominion beyond traditional domestic practices to include whatever activities become necessary in the new and strange circumstances.

Traill makes it clear in the section entitled "Apples" in *The Canadian Settler's Guide* that she anticipates the resistance of British women of her class to the notion of not just performing outdoor orchard work but in taking charge of the science of grafting, pruning, planting and fertilizing the orchard. Traill structures her response to these objections by the device of extending incrementally the domestic woman's traditional dominion over the home and all of its activities outward to the verandah, the surrounds of the house, the kitchen garden, the orchard, and later in the manual, to the forest itself. Armstrong notes that the domestic woman always exercised a form of power within the borders of her delineated domain, which was traditionally confined to the house.[29] Through the pages of *The Canadian Settler's Guide*, Traill adds more and more physical territory to that domain, and her consistent explanation for the necessity of this extension is that the activities she advocates are undertaken purely for the comfort, convenience, and care of her family. The hops growing up the verandah supports, the shrubbery, decorative creeping vines, and wild flowers transplanted from the forest to the yard, the vegetables and fruits that she grows, and the bounty gathered by the pioneer woman from the forest in the form of wild fruits, maple syrup and sugar, medicinal and cooking herbs, dyes for her wool, a coffee substitute and other edible wild foods, and the visual pleasure of wild flowers and greenery for Christmas decorations are all subsumed under the category of the domestic domain of the pioneer woman.

The conventions of domesticity become, for Traill, the larger and larger frame that increasingly subsumes more bits of the masculine domain and of masculine labour. She argues that if the pioneer wife is unwilling to undertake this work, her family will suffer the deprivation of these comforts alto-

gether. The reason for this is that the pioneer man is fully
occupied with his masculine sphere of work: "In Canada
where the heavy labour of felling trees and cultivating the
ground falls to the lot of the men, who have for some years
enough to do to clear ground to support the family and raise
means towards paying installments on the land, little leisure
is left for the garden and orchard: the consequence is that
these most necessary appendages to the farmhouse are either
totally neglected or left to the management of women and
children," Traill writes.[30] The masculine role is to pay off the
mortgage; he is the source of income for the family unit. The
feminine role (and domain of the increasingly expanding
domestic sphere) is to provide the comforts of life to the
family unit by spending as little money as possible, in order
to preserve the family's cash for land payments.[31]

But here, too, as the domestic space expands outward
from the house, it is the pioneer woman's qualities of mind
that ensure no loss of femininity, despite the outwardly masculine appearance of the activities she undertakes. Traill's calls
on what she refers to as "Female Energy" that allows a "weak
woman" to set her shoulder to "any kind of laborious work,"
even "tasks from which many men would have shrunk." But
she is careful to remark that the pioneer woman's physical
strength is laudable only because it is expended purely for
the benefit of others, particularly her children, and it is possible only because the domestic pioneer woman's internal
qualities prevail: her "strong will" and "energy of mind"
allow her to overcome her "natural weakness of body."[32] The
gentlewoman's class anxiety, too, is overcome by the qualities
of the mind in Traill's discussion of knitting. "To the mind of
the well-regulated female, there is no disgrace in so feminine
an occupation," she writes, "because in the colony knitting is
commonly done by ladies of her own rank."[33]

The cultural shift in emphasis noted by Armstrong
toward internal personal qualities rather than reliance on

external signs of social identity such as ostentatious display and inherited title gave rise to a new social need for self-regulation. Traill takes on the task of regulating the subjectivity of her self and the figure of the pioneer woman generally with vigor. Under her tutorship, the female readers of *The Canadian Settler's Guide* and *The Backwoods of Canada*, and Traill herself, may rest easy that the many trials and tribulations of pioneer life can be tackled with no distressing loss of gender or class identity. They are able to remain ladies.

That Traill's construction of the new pioneer woman's subjectivity contains some cracks only heightens our sense of the urgency of her cultural project. Traill's argument in *The Canadian Settler's Guide* of the necessity for enlarging the category of women's proper domestic practices to include work in the orchards and fields warns women of the possibility of the failure of the pioneer man to fulfill his side of the new sexual bargain in the homesteading family. In the section "Female Energy," she frankly says that the pioneer women may have to take on men's work because of "the indolence and inactivity of their husbands."[34] Similarly, in her discussion of orchards, Traill regrets the "miserable want of foresight" in the men's failure to appreciate the cash value of the orchard and garden produce, and their consequent neglect of cultivation in these areas. She notes that these crops are as valuable when sold as any other that the farm produces, and the clear implication of her remarks is that anything that produces cash ought rightfully to fall within the male domain of work. Traill's domestic category is infinitely flexible, growing in ever-increasing territorial rings moving incrementally outward from the house, but it also functions like a hovering sponge, ready to absorb any useful tasks that spill over from the male role.

If she reformulates femininity through her revision of the domestic fable, Traill also poses a more direct challenge to gender performance when she uses her pen to take on the task of naming the new world, an activity reserved for Adam in the Garden, not Eve. In her earliest work written as a settler, *The Backwoods of Canada*, she records her own carefree naming of wild plants: "As much of the botany of these unsettled portions of the country are unknown to the naturalist, and the plants quite nameless, I take the liberty of bestowing names upon them according to inclination or fancy," she writes.[35] She is perfectly aware of, but unapologetic about, her own transgressiveness in doing so: "I suppose our scientific botanists in Britain would consider me very impertinent in bestowing names on the flowers and plants I meet in these wild woods: I can only say, I am glad to discover the Canadian or even the Indian names if I can, and where I fail I consider myself free to become their floral godmother, and give them names of my own choosing."[36] Since the naming of plants is another piece of the traditional masculine domain that no man had at that time undertaken, Traill feels entitled to absorb the activity into her own arena of action. Naming is a part of the masculine logos of rational order that Traill takes upon herself in her sorting, cataloging, assigning the useful functions, and generally "cutting down to size" of the overwhelming wilderness experience.

But before the naming of plants, Traill was already engaged in the much more complex enterprise of naming her own experience, naming her self. Neither Traill herself nor the figure of the domestic pioneer woman in the Canadian wilderness that she creates can quite sustain an origin myth as the "mother of us all" for Canadian women. But if "floral godmother" is Traill's true legacy, it may be the only original Canadian myth that we have.

# Notes

1. *The Canadian Settler's Guide* (Toronto: McClelland and Stewart, 1969), reprint of *The Female Emigrant's Guide, and Hints on Canadian Housekeeping,* 1854.

2. Elizabeth Thompson, *The Pioneer Woman: A Canadian Character Type* (Montreal and Kingston: McGill-Queen's University Press, 1991).

3. T. D. MacLulich, "Crusoe in the Backwoods: A Canadian Fable?" *Mosaic,* Vol. 9 (1976), pp. 115-126.

4. *Ibid.,* p. 125.

5. Marion Fowler, *The Embroidered Tent: Five Gentlewomen in Early Canada* (Concord: Anansi, 1982), p. 84.

6. Gaile McGregor, *The Wacousta Syndrome: Explorations in Canadian Language* (Toronto: University of Toronto Press, 1985), p. 42.

7. Clara Thomas, *All My Sisters: Essays on the Work of Canadian Women Writers* (Ottawa: Tecumseh Press, 1994), p. 87.

8. Margaret Laurence, *The Diviners* (Toronto: Seal Books, 1974), p. 95.

9. *Ibid.,* p. 351.

10. *Ibid.,* p. 96.

11. *Ibid.,* p. 171.

12. *Ibid.,* p. 204.

13. Thompson, *op. cit.,* p. 156.

14. Carl P. A. Ballstadt, "Catharine Paar Traill," in Robert Lecker, Jack David and Ellen Quigley, eds. *Canadian Writers and Their Works* (Toronto: EWC, 1983), pp. 149-193.

15. Thompson, *op. cit.,* p. 31

16. *Ibid.,* pp. 170-173.

17. *Ibid.*

18. Catharine Paar Traill, *The Canadian Crusoes: A Tale of the Rice Lake Plains* (Ottawa: Carleton University Press, 1986).

19. Sigmund Freud, "Beyond the Pleasure Principle," in Peter Gay, ed., *The Freud Reader* (New York: W. W. Norton, 1989), pp. 599-600.

20. McGregor, *op. cit.,* p. 40.

21. Traill, *op. cit.,* p. 18.

22. Nancy Armstrong, *Desire and Domestic Fiction: A Political History of the Novel* (New York: Oxford University Press, 1987), p. 3.

23. *Ibid.,* p. 4.

24. *Ibid.,* pp. 4-5.

25. *Ibid.*, p. 3.

26. Traill, *op. cit.*, p. 1.

27. *Ibid.*, p. 9.

28. *Ibid.*, p. 10.

29. Armstrong, *op. cit.*, p. 19.

30. Traill, *op. cit.*, p. 58.

31. *Ibid.*, pp. 2, 22.

32. *Ibid.*, pp. 24-25.

33. *Ibid.*, p. 185.

34. *Ibid.*, p. 24.

35. Catharine Paar Traill, *The Backwoods of Canada: Being Letters from the Wife of an Emigrant Officer, Illustrative of the Domestic Economy of British America* (London: Charles Knight, 1836), p. 120.

36. *Ibid.*, pp. 143-144.

# Entertainment at the Front
# and at Home

A Postcolonial Study of "The Dumbells," 1917-1940

## Ches Skinner

During World War I, the Canadian soldiers stationed in Europe, and particularly in France, were treated to a popular form of entertainment known as "concert parties." One of the more significant groups that provided this necessary diversion was the Dumbells made up of Canada's Third Division (the name refers to that contingent's insignia). The Dumbells were one of thirty or more such groups active during 1916-1918. They performed music hall fare both at the front and at home. After the war, unlike so many other troupes, the men re-grouped and performed in most Canadian cities during fourteen very successful tours across the nation.

The Dumbells as a group is intriguing in that they survived for a decade after the Armistice. Their unique blend of European and Canadian experiences attests to the political and social developments at that time and illustrates the postcolonial paradigm and one of the first moves toward developing something Canadian while, at the same time, adhering to the model demanded by the centre.

In their book on the theory and practice in postcolonial literature entitled *The Empire Writes Back*, Ashcroft, Griffiths and Tiffin state:

During the imperial period [which Canada was at that time]
writing in the language of the imperial Centre [England] is
invariably produced by a literate elite whose primary identification is with the colonizing power. Such texts can never form
the basis for an indigenous culture, nor can they be integrated
in any way with the culture which already exists in the countries invaded [Canada]. Despite their detailed reportage of
landscape, custom and language, they inevitably privilege the
Centre, emphasizing the "home" over the "native," the metropolitan over the provincial and so forth.[1]

Although not entirely the same as written text, the theatre,
and in this case what the Dumbells did, are very similar and
in that they were using a formula and, to a great extent,
material which were inherited. The perseverance and almost
universal acceptance of the Dumbells after the war from
1920-1930 is due to some extent to the successful blend of
these elements within a countrywide fledgling nationalist
context. This essay will examine the work of the soldier-
actors and the factors that contributed to their fame, acceptance and eventual demise. First, it will look at their origin
and the political arena at that time in Europe and Canada,
and second it will consider their reception in Canada, particularly in the smaller communities where they were received
with great enthusiasm.

The story of the Dumbells begins in France amid the
almost incomprehensibly horrible conditions that enveloped
the soldiers fighting for the "good of the country." In what
essentially was a hand-to-hand combat, the Canadian soldiers,
like others fighting "the Hun," encountered a social and psychological landscape that stripped away any enthusiasm they
may have had when they enlisted in towns and villages back
home. In his account of the Canadian soldier in World War I,
Desmond Morton states:

Much about the war is inscrutable. The toughest question is
how men endured so much. The army had its inspirational

answers – *esprit de corps*, "comforts," discipline. The full truth
was as simple or as complex as the human spirit: all men had
limited heart, stomach, and stamina for battle. Among the many
labels for the symptoms of strain were "disordered action of the
heart" or, more commonly, "soldier's heart."[2]

The alleviation of this condition and the raising of morale
were the primary tasks of the Young Men's Christian
Association (YMCA). This organization played a significant
role in the conflict by providing some relief by way of its
recreation huts where soldiers could relax and avail themselves of basic amenities reminiscent of home. In addition to
magazines, books, games, pianos, gramophones, and cinema,
there was the concert party, an entertainment derived from
the English music hall tradition that included vaudeville and
minstrel routines, songs, sketches about army life, and most
popular of all, female impersonations–all with the intent of
providing a respite through laughter.

Early in the war English performers provided the front
line entertainment free but, as the conflict wore on, it
became necessary to charge a fee. And the YMCA obliged by
footing the bill for this activity for the remainder of the war-
to the tune of $681,000.00.[3]

In France, however, there was no pool of professional
English performers. There the entertainment depended on
the discovery and use of talent within the army which,
according to most accounts, suffered from a limited repertoire and a standard of taste imposed by the Command and
the YMCA that forbade anything objectionable. And most
were impromptu! To supplement locally grown fare, the
organized concert or concert party was introduced using
suitably talented men who had enlisted as soldiers. These
events soon became an inextricable feature of life in the
Canadian Corps.

The person responsible for the highly proficient
Canadian concert parties was Capt. Merton Plunkett, an

experienced entertainment manager from Ontario, who's captaincy was with the YMCA rather than the military. Although Plunkett organized a number of such performance groups, it was the Dumbells that was most enduring. Groups such as the Y Emmas, the Maple Leafs, the Woodpeckers, Whizz Bangs, *Rouge et Noir*, the See Toos, Princess Patricia Light Infantry Company, and the Canadian Scottish Concert Party eventually disbanded with some of the better performers being absorbed by the Dumbells.

Concert parties became such an important part of the morale boosting endeavour that a training centre known as "the Dramatic School" was established where Capt. Plunkett trained the various troupes in routines and outfitted them with costumes and simple scenery pieces.

The concert factory, as it was sometimes called, was turning out parties at such a rate during the winter of 1917-1918 that before spring there were nineteen of them on the YMCA list. With these and other parties organized by divisions touring the various units of the Canadian Corps, there were entertainments every evening within reach of almost every unit. During the quiet months of the winter of 1918, entertainment on the front in France reached its height. Even after the troubled days of spring and summer set in, it continued on a large scale. In September, 1918, for example, a month in which the Canadians were in constant action against the famous Hindenberg Line, the statistics show that seventy-one concerts were presented and one hundred and seventy-nine cinema performances were held with a total attendance of seventy-seven thousand soldiers.[4]

The Dumbells, started in 1917, became the standard. Under Plunkett's guidance, some skillful management and "being in the right place at the right time," they traveled throughout France and, on October 17, 1917, they officially opened the new Pavilion Theatre built at the Canadian Corps Training School (Dramatic School). They created such an impression that the Dumbells were installed as the permanent entertainment company serving to train others. Further cementing the fame of the 3$^{rd}$ Division party was a trip to London where these soldiers from the colony gave a number of performances at St. James and The Apollo theatres as well as hospitals and YMCA centres.

The success of the Dumbells can be attributed to two factors. First, under Capt. Plunkett's experienced tutelage, they became the trainers and therefore were able to establish and perfect the formulae. Second, their relative success in the imperial centre was of paramount importance in ensuring their place in the company was accepted. With Canada being a major part of the British Empire and within the colonial framework, it was necessary that the model be English and that Canada's attempts at literature and the arts be as close as possible to the imperial paradigm. Therefore, the reputation of the Canadian troupe was authenticated when they played to appreciative audiences in London, even garnering an invitation to play at Windsor Castle. Following their trip to London and a stint entertaining British forces, the Dumbells finished out the war with some seventy or more shows including a successful production of *HMS Pinafore*.

Shortly after the armistice the Dumbells returned to Canada, but a Canada different from the one they left. In order to understand the reason for their success back home, it is necessary to examine the changes that had occurred. During the war years Canada had made the move from colony to independence. The soldiers had developed an identity as Canadians distinct from Great Britain and took glory from their valour and victories, especially at Vimy Ridge. By the end of the European conflict the Canadian politicians were reconstructing a nation with a role to play in international affairs, and nationalism and patriotism were words in the language as people took pride and ownership in the accomplishments realized in Europe.

As well, the country was moving from a rural society to one centred in urban areas. Land was no longer as available and people found work in the cities in the factories that had sprung up to supply the war machine. This demographic change played an important role in the subsequent tour of the Dumbells in that they announced that they would visit only the larger centres; this therefore gave those cities on the itinerary a sense of having joined the big leagues. The country was rich. The price of wheat had doubled. Lumber and mining had increased considerably. A new industrial economy was emerging. And the soldiers who comprised the Dumbells continued doing what they had done for three years. They re-organized under the management of Capt. Plunkett and brought Canadians the product they had provided for the men at the front. However, before their cross-country tour, the Dumbells established their reputation in the larger cities of Ontario, and to cap it off for this postcolonial society, they performed on Broadway – a feat of equal significance to the London enterprise.

So, armed with their European experience and the success of playing the Great White Way, the Dumbells took their show from sea to sea playing to sold-out houses along the way. They were billed as actor-soldiers and much was made of the fact that, in addition to entertaining the troops in France, they had fought in the trenches. Headlines in the local newspapers were always positive from the early visits in 1920 to those in 1930; for example, "Dumbells – All Soldiers Remember Them" (1920), "Dumbells Are as Pleasing as Ever" (1925), "Joy Bombs Explode Barrage of Real Fun" (1927), "Dumbells Are as Bright and Breezy as Ever" (1929). Often the news items were copied verbatim from the company's press releases with identical texts appearing in several newspapers. Perhaps indicative of the kind of attention accorded to the Dumbells is this one from 1920:

Biff! Bing! Bang! is the catchy title of the original overseas musical comedy review which the famous "Dumbells" are offering here. The "Dumbells" as they were called in France where they gave over 500 performances to our Canadian soldiers, is an organization of soldier-actors who were chosen by Capt. Plunkett from practically every branch of the service. Every member of the cast and chorus has a record of at least sixteen months' service to his credit before joining the entertainment corps . . . Their performance, while given entirely by soldiers, is along similar lines to the big musical revues so much in vogue in London and New York and the boys play everything from chorus girls to prima donnas. The costumes and scenery are the last word in gorgeousness and the many song and dance numbers, most of which were written especially for them by some of England's best composers are brilliantly sung and executed.[5]

That excerpt is typical of the response to the "boys from France" in other towns. It in many ways encapsulates the reasons for that response. They were, according to the paper, "our boys," the outside world had agreed that they were good, and some of their material had even been written by "England's best composers," thus fulfilling the major tenets of the postcolonial paradigm. The fact that they were Canadian soldiers validated the performance by lending a degree of authority to this activity which was usually marginalized in most rural and some urban centres. In particular, it gave the seal of approval to the appearance of Margie, the popular character that had been a part of the Dumbells' repertoire from the beginning, as expressed in this 1920 commentary in *The Lethbridge Herald*:

Ask any soldier to tell you the name of the most famous girl in France and he will smile and answer Margie. Now, "Margie" was the leading "lady" of the finest bunch of all soldier talent ever gathered together to entertain the boys while they were in the rest billets just behind the lines, and her makeup was so perfect that many believed her to be a famous actress smuggled up to no man's land in the guise of a private soldier. This

is true in a measure, as "Marjorie" did go up as a common soldier and remained there for sixteen months.[6]

In addition to the connection to authority and the image of
the military, the Dumbells appear to have been good performers as singers, dancers, actors and musicians. Plunkett,
the consummate manager, combined the "best of the best" of
all the groups at the end of the war and, according to the
various reviews in Canada, they delivered a product befitting
the reputation that they had developed in Europe. Also con-
tributing to their success is the fact that they produced a
number of records of their songs.

The Dumbells made fourteen trips across Canada and,
according to the press, "they always left audiences wanting
more" and promised to return with a bigger and better production. The core of the group remained constant with new
performer-soldiers added as people dropped out. By 1930
there appears to be some indication in the press of fatigue
creeping in, with the press releases reassuring audiences that
the program had changed. In fact, in the 1930 show, Plunkett
included women in the troup – the Dumbellettes.

The demise of the Dumbells is not unrelated to those
same factors that gave them their fame. The war had been
over for more than a decade. The soldiers who were heroes
upon their return had lost some of that status and, in many
cases, they discovered that the promise they had fought and
hoped for did not materialize. They, and most of society, had
moved on to other things. One of the biggest factors that led
to the demise of the Old Dumbells, as they were called in
the later part of the decade, was the Depression which ended
the prosperity that had allowed the accommodation of such
diversions as theatre.

The Dumbells regrouped in 1940, but it was a short-
lived revival and plans to perform again for the soldiers in
Europe were never realized. The Dumbells emerged at a time

of cultural transition in which colonial attitudes were struggling with a new sense of national identity and independence. They gave expression to that process, but times had
changed; new rules were being adopted and the Dumbells
were by then a thing of the past.

## Notes

1. Bill Ashcroft, Gareth Griffiths and Helen Tiffin, *The Empire
Writes Back* (London: Routledge & Kegan Paul, 1989), p. 5.

2. Desmond Morton, *When Your Number's Up* (Toronto: Random
House of Canada, 1993), p. 227.

3. Charles Bishop, *The Canadian Y.M.C.A. in the Great War*
(Toronto: Y.M.C.A., 1921), p. 158.

4. *Ibid.*, pp. 155-156.

5. *The Lethbridge Herald* (20 February, 1920), p. 14.

6. *The Lethbridge Herald* (25 February, 1920), p. 5.

# Were Theatre Musicians Luddites?

## The Arrival of Sound Film in Canada

## Douglas Bailie

In July, 1930, when the manager of Keith's theatre in Ottawa decided to eliminate vaudeville performance at his theatre and run an "all-talkie" motion picture program, the unionized musicians refused to accept termination of their jobs. For the remaining six weeks of their contract, they took their places in the orchestra pit as usual. They never played a note and the "occupation of the pit" failed to pressure the management into bringing back vaudeville.[1]

This incident is one of several that could be used to show the fruitless opposition of Canadian musicians to sound film and their stubborn refusal to accept the changes recorded sound brought to commercial theatre. A more distinctly Luddite note was sounded at the annual convention of the Trades and Labour Congress of Canada in 1932 when a resolution was passed "urging local labour bodies to support demands for the abolition of mechanical music in theatres."[2]

But these provide only a selective view of musicians' response to the arrival of sound film. In fact there was no consistent response from the musicians; negotiations for severance pay, strikes for job security, campaigns against "mechanical music," and attempts to find new jobs for musicians in the era of recorded sound all took place. A clearer historical view of this issue requires a critical

approach to the commonly held perception that the arrival
of sound film and the elimination of silent film was a simple case of technological progress; that is, once the technology of sound was developed, the end of silent film was
inevitable; the motion picture industry was just giving people what they wanted.

Sound film certainly was popular, and if this was all there
was to the story, then the fate of theatre musicians would
have been a fairly simple matter as well. With the disappearance of silent films, the musicians that provided accompani-
ment for those films would all be quickly out of jobs.
Instead, many musicians found themselves in and out of
work in the years following the arrival of the talkies as theatre managers tried to figure out what kind of show would
most likely draw crowds. While the response of unionized
musicians to the arrival of sound film was at times reac-
tionary, it is not surprising that they would use what collective strength they still had to maintain as many jobs as possible. Also, the role of corporations in theatre suggests that
the arrival of sound was not a simple case of technological
progress, and therefore opposition to it was not simply a
reaction to innovation.

Before the sound revolution, motion pictures were often
presented along with other live acts. Generally speaking, only
small neighbourhood theatres showed nothing but film.
Many theatres, and especially the palatial downtown theatres,
included musical numbers and various other acts either
before the films or in between the shorts and the main feature. When attendance was lagging, theatre managers would
sometimes try to win the public back by boosting their stage
shows. In the 1920s, an increasingly popular form of theatre
was the "combination house"– a theatre that combined five
or six acts of vaudeville with a feature film. These programs
constituted added value for the customer, and that meant the
tickets cost a little more. But people were willing to pay

extra when they went downtown, and they expected to be entertained accordingly.

None of this changed with the arrival of sound film that made its debut in Canada at the Palace in Montreal. The musical "prologue" was seen so much as a key part of the show that, a couple of weeks after the debut, the Palace's manager expanded the size of the orchestra as part of an augmented stage show.[3] But how long would such lavish productions last? Certainly, they were never even considered for the smaller theatres that dispensed with their musicians as soon as their sound equipment was installed. But that fact may have made some downtown theatre managers even more reluctant to do away with their orchestras, because sound film made it possible for the neighbourhood theatres to feature extravagant orchestral numbers. How would downtown theatres continue to distinguish their programs from the neighbourhood theatres?

Several of the combination theatres were unable to make a clean break with live performances. Famous Players' theatres first discontinued stage shows in the spring of 1930. This was apparently intended to be permanent, but new shows were restarted in the fall.[4] Another example is the Keith theatre in Ottawa which adopted sound in April, 1929 and discontinued vaudeville two months later. The following September, vaudeville was reintroduced, only to be abandoned again in May, 1930.[5] Similarly, the Imperial theatre in Montreal abandoned vaudeville in September, 1930, only to bring it back the following March. This change was reported in the *Canadian Moving Pictures Digest* by saying that the policy of showing only films at the Imperial had put the theatre "far into the red, even with double-featured bills."[6]

Theatre managers continued to change their programs because the possibility of eliminating live performances was such an attractive idea. Take, for example, Loew's theatre in Toronto, a combination vaudeville and film house. In its first year with sound film, net revenue increased by over 60%. Loew's then dropped vaudeville from its program. Not only would the theatre no longer have to pay for traveling performers, but at the same time it eliminated the bulk of its organizational work force – the musicians and the stage hands. On top of that, it maintained the same ticket prices. As long as the public was willing to go along with such changes, which they were in the case of Loew's, the positive effect on profit margins could be substantial in the long term.[7]

So it is clear why theatre managers wanted to eliminate live performances, but their audiences did not always accept this. The fact that many theatres had to backtrack indicates that the public still expected live performances.

Over a period of a few years, however, almost all forms of live commercial theatre in Canada were eliminated. As a result, between 1929 and 1933, I would estimate that about 3,000 theatre musicians lost their jobs. The membership of the American Federation of Musicians (AFM), as reported by the Dominion Bureau of Statistics (DBS), provides the best source for this estimate because most theatre musicians in Canada, as in the United States, were unionized. But the numbers are inconclusive because they were reported as estimates rather than precise numbers, and also because a large number of AFM members did not make a living as full-time musicians. So, while AFM membership was reported to have been cut in half, from 8,000 to 4,000 between 1929 and 1933, and while almost all of the losses likely came from theatres, it would be prudent to round down the number of lost theatre jobs from 4,000 to 3,000.[8] Another source that supports this estimate is an article in the *Toronto Telegram* that counted 300 jobs lost by the city's theatre musicians by 1930.[9] Considering that the number of theatres in Toronto was equal to about 10% of the total number of theatres in Canada (ninety-eight in Toronto, nine hundred and seventy-five in all of Canada),[10] then we can extrapolate that the sound revolution would eventually affect about 3,000 musicians across the country.

There is little reason to believe that these job losses were offset by new jobs for musicians in other areas. The *Telegram* article mentioned above noted that jobs in radio did not come close to making up for the losses in theatres in Toronto. James Kraft's study of musicians in the United States shows that, while about 20,000 theatre musicians lost their jobs in the early 1930s, only about 1,000 were working in radio in 1935, and most of those jobs were with one of the networks. In Canada,[11] according to the *Labour Gazette*, 250 musicians worked for the Canadian Radio Broadcasting Commission when the network was hit by a strike in 1934.[12] The AFM membership in Canada did not show any signs of growth again until the mid-1930, reported by the DBS as 5,000 in 1936.[13]

Thus, some theatre musicians moved into radio, and some would have found other ways of making a living by their talent, such as working in dance bands. But for most it meant the end of their professional musical careers, and joining the ranks of the unemployed in the Depression. The jobs they lost had paid them better than most workers in Canada. In 1928, when the average wage in Canada was about $20 per week, musicians at small neighbourhood theatres in Toronto received $24 to $28, while those at the downtown theatres owned by Famous Players received $65.

Unemployed musicians were not simply a side-effect of sound. Warner Bros. Studio was the first to invest in sound because it was convinced not only of the potential popularity of recorded sound but also because of the business advantages of eliminating orchestras, both in theatres they owned and those independents to whom they rented films. In 1925, when Warners first began producing sound films, it was not in the top tier of Hollywood Studios. Although the technology for

sound films had been established in the early 1920s, the top
studios had shown little interest in something that had the
potential to make a large part of their business obsolete.
Warners had less to lose, and new technology offered an
opportunity for it to become a leading studio. Reducing
labour costs was one of the main reasons for adopting the new
technology.[14]

In June, 1928, the annual convention of the AFM discussed the problem of "canned" music. The strategy they
chose was to mount an advertising campaign which would
educate the public as to the superiority of "living music" and
encourage the public to pressure theatre managers to include
five live performances in their programs. Over the next two
years, the union spent $1.2 million on the campaign. About
three million people declared their support for the musicians
by signing the Musical Defense League coupons that they
clipped out of the print ads and mailed to the union.[15]

It is interesting to note that a minority opinion at the
convention argued in favour of a recording boycott. They
made the obvious point that recorded music still required
musicians; it could not replace musicians the way other forms
of technology had replaced industrial workers, but it did
severely reduce the number of musicians the theatre industry
required. A recording boycott was eventually used with a fair
degree of success in the 1940s. But in the late 1920s and
early 1930s, the union's president, Joseph Weber, argued that
such action would hold the AFM up to ridicule. Instead, he
argued, the union should concentrate on gaining public support for live musical performances.[16]

Such a campaign was inherently flawed. First, it represented a typical elitist critique of popular culture: that
unique, local events are always superior to those that are
reproduced through the mass media. This argument would
not likely convince many members of the public who had
had access to recorded sound for years through radio or

record players. These media had exposed local audiences to the works of musicians from cultural centres like New York and London and, if anything, had increased the public's standards; so the musicians' attempt to portray themselves as defenders of culture likely sounded self-serving. Second, most theatre musicians' jobs were created by motion pictures. For them now to turn around and denounce mass media was entirely disingenuous.

The union was, in fact, trying to walk a fine line; Weber argued that it was pointless to oppose technological innovation, and instead tried to emphasize the positive value of live music. Therefore, Weber's goal was not to bring an end to all recorded music, simply to re-establish as many theatre orchestras as possible.[17] Nevertheless, the campaign often described recorded music in hostile terms – a 1929 resolution referred to recorded sound as "a profanation of the art of music"[18] – which must have undermined the union's credibility.

I have not found much evidence that Canadian locals pursued this campaign with any vigour, with the exception of Montreal's Musicians' Protective Association (AFM Local 406). Beginning in August, 1930, a series of free concerts, sponsored by the Montreal Trades and Labor Council, were held in public parks with the aim of educating the public about music and to employ musicians. The TLC president, J. T. Foster, said: "Ultimately the public will rebel against mechanical music and we shall have the human element back in the theatre."[19] In Montreal's Labour Day parade, in front of the band a banner was carried, reading "This Is Not Canned Music." Another banner read "While Canned Music Is Making a Racket, Musicians Starve." Note that the rhetoric pitted workers against machines – clearly a message associated with Luddism.

While the musicians were protesting, Famous Players was planning the debut of its new stage shows – touring units produced by Famous Players' parent company,

Paramount-Publix – which would be featured at Montreal's Capitol theatre. The contract Famous Players offered the musicians included a pay raise, but the musicians also wanted job security – that is, a firm commitment from the company that the orchestra would be maintained at the Capitol for a full year. Famous Players wanted to be able to cancel the contract with two weeks' notice. The *Canadian Moving Picture Digest* described the union's hard line as "somewhat of a bombshell" considering the high unemployment among the city's musicians. With no agreement, the sixteen musicians at the Capitol walked off the job on 1 September, 1930.[20]

Two weeks later, the orchestras at three other Famous Players' theatres struck in sympathy. In total, thirty-eight musicians were affected by the strike. The manager of the Imperial, one of the theatres involved, said that the strike only anticipated the elimination of vaudeville at his theatre, and therefore "no negotiations for the musicians' return will be made."[21] On 1 October, the musicians returned to the orchestra pits at three of the four theatres. A compromise deal settled the situation at the Capitol. The contract could be cancelled following four weeks notice, a right that the theatre's management exercised a few months later. The orchestra at the Imperial was merged with that at Loew's, until vaudeville was revived again at the Imperial the following February.[22]

While the strike was underway, Montreal sent delegates to the Trades and Labour Congress convention in Regina, where they introduced a resolution calling on the government in increase the tax on the imposition of sound equipment to encourage its manufacture in Canada. Supporters of the resolution felt it was reasonable given the number of musicians thrown out of work by sound equipment. Others felt it would only increase ticket prices. Rather than defeat the motion outright, it was referred to the executive for further study and never heard of again.[23]

Of more lasting consequence were a series of concerts staged by Montreal's unemployed musicians in the fall of 1930. Unlike the free, open-air concerts in the summer, tickets were sold and there was enough public support to keep them going. Thus begins the history of the Montreal Symphony Orchestra.

The Montreal musicians used traditional union tactics, such as the strike, to maintain as many theatre orchestras as possible. The strategy had a degree of success. But it was only temporary, as the popularity of sound film and the determination of the theatre managers to eliminate live performances won in the end. The unions attempt, with the support of the Trades and Labor Council, to build audience demand for live music had little positive effect.

Union tactics in Edmonton, on the other hand, showed a direct attempt to find a role for local musicians in the era of sound. In the spring of 1929, after the Capitol and Empress theatres installed sound equipment and got rid of their orchestras, management was asked to hire members of the musicians' union to control the volume during sound films and operate the non-synchronous sound system. (The non-sync machine was a record player that could be used whenever the theatre needed music, but no musicians were on duty).

The managers of the Capitol and the Empress, Famous Players' main theatres in downtown Edmonton, thought the suggestion of hiring musicians at $55 per week to control the volume during the talkies and to take care of the non-sync machine was a ludicrous idea. But it was one they could not easily disregard, because the request to hire the musicians did not come from the now powerless musicians' union, but from the increasingly powerful projectionists' union.[24]

Facing a strike that almost certainly would have forced them to close their theatres' doors, the managers agreed to arbitration under Alberta's *Labour Disputes Act*. In their testi-

mony to the arbitration board, Walter Wilson of the Capitol
and K. G. Findlay of the Empress explained that the volume
level during sound films was routinely regulated by either the
manager or the assistant manager, who stood at the back of
the theatre and sent signals to the projection booth via an
electronic bell. As for the non-sync machine, neither the
Capitol nor the Empress had any use for it. Wilson and
Findlay also produced statements from other theatres to
attest to the bizarre nature of the union's request, and to
establish that this was not a common practice. A statement
from H. M. Thomas, Famous Players' regional manager for
Western Canada, said, "I do not recall where we now employ
anyone to regulate sound volume for us in any of our theatres as this would be a very silly procedure."[25]

Union representatives, however, showed the board evidence that several theatres across Western Canada, including
some Famous Players' theatres, hired musicians for precisely
this purpose. Furthermore, the idea to make such a contract
demand did not come from the Edmonton locals but was
directed by the international union headquarters in New
York, suggesting that similar demands were being made
across the United States and Canada. The discrepancy
between union and management evidence on this point of
fact was raised by the board but never resolved.

What was really at issue were two points of view of
technology and work; although the board's hearings avoided
debating points of principle, the employers saw this as a case
of union featherbedding, while the union refused to accept
that new technology must lead to redundant workers.
Fortunately for the board, they were able to avoid passing
judgement. A compromise was reached, with the intervention
of the AFM president, Joseph Weber, whereby the orchestra
at the Empire theatre – a legitimate theatre, and yet another
Famous Players' house – would be increased by two. In
return, the unions would make no further demands for

employing musicians at the Empress or Capitol for the purposes of controlling sound equipment. This was a satisfactory compromise in that two musicians gained meaningful employment; however, within a year the orchestra at the Empire was itself out of work.[26]

Clearly, the redundancy of theatre musicians resulted not only from the decline of silent film but also that of vaudeville and legitimate theatre. To understand this process fully, we must discuss Famous Players' role in the disappearance of live commercial theatre. Famous Players was a subsidiary of Paramount, the most powerful Hollywood studio of the times, and the only Canada-wide chain of motion picture theatres between the early 1920s and 1940s. In addition, it was affiliated with most regional or local chains and dominated film distribution in Canada. This meant that even most independent theatres were beholden to Famous Players. A federal government investigation under the *Combines Act* in 1932 concluded that Famous Players had been in a monopoly position in the Canadian motion picture market since at least 1926.[27]

Famous Players' control of legitimate theatres like the Empire in Edmonton was extensive by the late 1920s. What was left of vaudeville came under its control with the creation in 1930 of the RKO-Canada chain – a partnership between Radio-Keith-Orpheum and Famous Players. Not surprisingly, those who were disturbed by the gradual disappearance of live theatre blamed Famous Players. A key part of their argument was that Famous Players was responsible for making it uneconomical for acts to tour in Canada by converting theatres from live to motion picture venues. With fewer houses in which to play, and greater distances to travel between each booking, acts could no longer afford to tour Canada.[28]

But was this a fair criticism? Certainly there were other reasons for the decline of touring performers, such as increasing transportation costs and the reluctance of theatre managers to raise ticket prices to cover those costs.[29] But the most obvious question is why would Famous Players bother creating a vaudeville chain in 1930 if it was not interested in vaudeville? The answer is the short history of RKO–Canada itself. It began with only eight theatres, stretching from coast to coast. Within a year, most of these theatres were almost exclusively motion picture theatres.[30] Famous Players was never interested in maintaining vaudeville. It was, however, interested in obtaining control of some of the prime theatre spaces in Canada, and that was what it got out of the RKO chain.

To summarize, the elimination of the theatre musician did not follow immediately upon the arrival of sound film. It came only after a transitional period in which all forms of commercial live theatre were almost entirely eliminated, which in itself requires audiences to adjust their expectations. Theatre managers claimed that all these changes were a simple matter of giving audiences what they wanted. But the industry was also manipulating consumer demand in a way that ultimately reduced consumer choices and strengthened Famous Players' dominance of the Canadian market. In this light, the musicians' attempts to defend their interest as workers were reasonable, even though the strategies they chose were often flawed. The attempt to reshape theatres by managers, owners and the vertically-integrated industry of which they were part succeeded not only because of the strength of capital over labour but also because of its success in claiming the support of the mass audience – the same support the musicians tried but failed to harness.

# Notes

1. *Canadian Moving Picture Digest* (5 July, 6 September, 1930), hereafter *Digest*.

2. Department of Labour, *Labour Gazette* (1932), p. 1065.

3. *Digest* (1 September, 29 September, 1928).

4. *Ibid.* (19 April, 26 July, 1930).

5. *Ibid.* (22 June, 31 August, 1929; 31 May, 1930).

6. *Ibid.*, (4 October, 1930; 28 February, 1931); *Montreal Gazette* (1 October, 1930).

7. *Digest* (3 May, 1930).

8. Dominion Bureau of Statistics, *The Canada Year Book* (Ottawa: Government of Canada, 1931), p. 759; 1934-1935, p. 814.

9. *Toronto Telegram* (27 September, 1930).

10. *Digest* (30 November, 1929; 29 March, 6 September, 1930); *Canada Year Book,* 1940.

11. James P. Kraft, *Stage to Studio: Musicians and the Studio Revolution* (Baltimore: Johns Hopkins University Press, 1996), p. 33, 73.

12. *Labour Gazette*, 1934, p. 625.

13. *Canada Year Book*, 1938, p. 742. The membership remains at 5,000 in 1937 and 1938: see 1939, p. 790 and 1940, p. 772.

14. Kraft, *op. cit.*, p. 48.

15. *Ibid.*, pp 51-54.

16. Robert D. Leiter, *The Musicians and the Petrillo* (New York: Bookman Associates, 1953), p. 60; Kraft, *op. cit.*, p. 51.

17. Kraft, *op. cit.*, pp. 51-52.

18. *Digest* (8, 15 June, 1929).

19. *Ibid.* (16 August, 1930).

20. *Ibid.* (6 September, 1930); *Labour Gazette* (1930), p. 1138.

21. *Digest* (4 October, 1930).

22. *Ibid.* (18 October, 1930; 17 January, 1931; 28 February, 1931); *Labour Gazette* (1930), p. 1138.

23. *Ibid.* (20 September, 1930). The resolution was not mentioned in the TLC's report on the Regina convention in the *Canadian Congress Journal* (October, 1930).

24. The projectionists' union (IATSE, Local 360) was joined in the demand by the stagehands' (IATSE, Local 210). *Labour Gazette* (1929), p. 1205; PAA, *Premiers' Papers*, File 365, "In the Matter of the *Labour Disputes Act*, 1926" and "A Dispute between Capitol and Empress (employers) Theatres and Locals 360 and 210, I.A.T.S.E. (Employees")," Edmonton, Alberta, Sept. 24, 1929."

25. PAA, *Premiers' Papers*, File 365, telegram from H. M. Thomas, Winnipeg, to W. Wilson, 25 September, 1929.

26. *Ibid. Edmonton Journal* (1 October, 1929). A survey of the *Journal*'s theatre pages in 1930 shows the Empire was dark most of that year.

27. Peter White, *Investigations into an Alleged Combine in the Motion Picture Industry in Canada* (Ottawa: Department of Labour, 1931).

28. A series of articles on this subject appeared in *Saturday Night* (26 July; 2, 9 and 23 August; 13 September; and 25 October, 1930).

29. For an in-depth look at this question, see Jack Poggi, *Theater in America: The Impact of Economic Forces, 1870-1967* (Ithaca: Cornell University Press, 1968), pp. 28-43.

30. White, *op. cit.*, p. 110.

# Social Transformation
# and Canadian Visual Art

## A Study of Lisa Neighbour's
## "Illuminations" Exhibition

## Gordon Hatt

Then, turning round his great eye, he discerned the strangers, and growled out to them, demanding who they were, and where from. Ulysses replied most humbly, stating that they were Greeks, from the great expedition that had lately won so much glory in the conquest of Troy; that they were now on their way home, and finished by imploring his hospitality in the name of the gods. Polyphemus deigned no answer, but reaching out his hand seized two of the Greeks, whom he hurled against the side of the cave, and dashed out their brains. He proceeded to devour them with great relish, and having made himself a hearty meal, stretched himself out on the floor to sleep.[1]

In his 1993 year-end review of Toronto visual art, writer and artist Oliver Girling gave pride of place to Lisa Neighbour's exhibition "In the Dark," calling it "Dazzling." Girling, however, didn't merely praise the work, but praised it in contrast to what he perceived to be a dominant trend in art at that time – art that was, in his words, "cynical, smarty-pants, self-referential."[2] And so it was, in those years of the early 1990s: pessimism did at times give way to cynicism. The Canadian art world was experiencing a malaise; indeed all of Canada was in the dumps by the end of 1993. The economy was in terrible shape and struggling to recover from the recession of 1990. The effects of free trade with the United States and the rapid development of a global marketplace were traumatizing and painful. Canadian cultural identity, founded in the post-war period on universal health care, state-owned industries and government support for education and culture, was coming apart at the seams as both provincial and federal governments were facing debt crises. Ontario's social democratic NDP government was in a battle with its traditional supporters, the public service unions, to renegotiate contracts in exchange for job security – the so-called Social Contract. Program spending in areas of heath, education and culture was being frozen or cut back at all levels of government.

By 1990, it was estimated that nine million people were infected with HIV worldwide. The effects of global warming and ozone depletion threatened an ecological disaster of unimaginable proportions. In 1993, the largest and longest-sustained hole in the ozone layer was recorded – 25 million square kilometres – larger than the European continent.[3] The psychic relief from the end of the cold war, the dissolution of the Soviet Union and the reduced threat of nuclear war were tempered by the realization that international market values now reigned supreme and that there was no foreseeable alternative to global capitalism.

Visual art sustained particularly intense attacks in the early 1990s. In the United States, controversy over the work of Andres Serrano and Robert Mapplethorpe, and in Canada, the National Gallery's acquisition of Barnett Newman's *Voice of Fire* and Mark Rothko's *No. 16*, focused debate on government support for the arts. In New York, the 1993 Whitney Biennial, which received scathing reviews in the mainstream press, seemed to define the chasm that had opened up between the art world and an uncomprehending and increasingly recalcitrant public.[4]

In Toronto, the confusion came to a head when artist Eli

Langer was prosecuted for the alleged crime of producing child pornography, stemming from his exhibition of paintings and drawings at the artist-run gallery Mercer Union. Buffeted by recession and the collapse of the commercial art market and stung by the erosion of public support for the arts, the arts community was on the defensive. Faced with the dystopic prospect of a rampant killer disease and a global ecological meltdown, the humanistic belief that underpinned the arts community – that an enlightened society could develop rationally, humanely and free of exploitation – was foundering on a pervasive sense of pessimism and gloom. Los Angeles curator and critic Ralph Rugoff coined the term "Pathetic Art" for work by emerging artists that reflected feelings of failure, powerlessness and inadequacy.[5] In an article in the *New Yorker*, Adam Gopnik identified the emergence of a new "Moribund Manner," wherein he perceived the building of "memorials-in-advance to an apocalypse whose causes are ill-defined but whose inevitability is grimly certain."[6] Death and despair, it seems, had become the metaphors for the life we were living in the early 1990s.

Toronto's Queen Street West in the 1980s was an artists' community not unlike the Lower East Side community of artists in New York during the same period, where young, middle-class, art school graduates lived in a socially distressed, working-class, ethnic ghetto. Such neighbourhoods were primarily attractive for their cheap flats or rough commercial/industrial spaces-ideal for artists who wanted a situation in which to live and work.

In 1981, Lisa Neighbour and her partner Carlo Cesta moved into an old, six-story industrial building at 620 Richmond Street West. "Six-Twenty Richmond," as it was known, was a short block from the busy corner of Queen and Bathurst Streets. It was a mixed industrial commercial, residential neighbourhood with Eastern European and Portuguese enclaves. But as Toronto recovered from the recession of the early 1980s, Queen Street West started to become trendy. 620 Richmond was renovated, rents were increased, and Lisa Neighbour and Carlo Cesta were forced to move further west into the community of Parkdale.

After graduating from the Ontario College of Art in 1981, Neighbour and a few school friends had established a print shop in the basement of her mother's house in midtown Toronto. For the next four years she worked as a waitress in the evenings and traveled uptown to make prints during the day. She started to show her work at the Angel Art Gallery on Avenue Road, owned by Nan Shuttleworth. But by the mid-1980s Neighbour was beginning to experience a crisis of motivation. A period of living in New York exposed her to frontline issues in contemporary art and caused her to lose faith in the body of work she had been developing since graduating from art school. The positive feedback that she had received from her exhibitions at the Angel Art Gallery no longer seemed sufficient cause to make art. Her frustration and unhappiness at this creative block was reflected in work that was increasingly dark and angry. A couple of years after moving from 620 Richmond to Parkdale, she decided that, "What I needed to do was something just for me and not for anybody else."[7] Neighbour returned to an experience that she had in her former neighbourhood for inspiration:

> I discovered it almost by accident. I was watching a construction crew setting up the lights on the church at Adelaide and Bathurst Streets for the Portuguese festival. It was beautiful to see happening. They would link up each piece with the wires, up there swinging from these dangerous looking scaffolds. At some point somebody would throw the big switch and it would go on.[8]

St. Mary's Catholic Church (Santa Maria) at the corner of Adelaide and Bathurst was elaborately decorated every year for the Portuguese community's festival of *Senhor Santo Cristo dos Milagres*, as was St. Ines Catholic Church (Santa Ines) at Dundas and Grace for the festival of *Senhor da Pedra*. The decorations consisted of images painted on plywood and laced with strings of coloured lights, each connected to the next with flowers and garlands. The festivals at St. Mary's and St. Ines were a religious *Gesamtkunstwerk* uniting folk art, religion and community.

Part of the attraction the church decorations held for Neighbour came from her interest in "outsider" art. In Canada, the critique of social power that began in the 1960s continued to influence the changing cultural landscape. Advocates of feminism, multi-culturalism, aboriginal rights and gay rights continued to question the existing structures of authority and privilege. In the visual arts, the imposing edifice of Clement Greenberg's post-war modernism started to come undone as a result of this critique, and many artists began to investigate domestic, folk and naïve art forms as alternative modes of expression and as symbols of cultural resistance.[9]

And folk art seemed fresher, less affected and free of that tiresome academic cant. Neighbour's partner, Carlo Cesta had exhibited his work at Claude Arsenault's Home Again Gallery in 1981 and 1983, a gallery that specialized in folk art. Neighbour, moreover, had considerable experience with Mexican folk art, having been to Mexico with her family frequently over the years. Mexican folk religion, its festival decoration and its votive shrines, often made with whatever material was available, became a significant influence not only on the body of work she was now developing, but also as part of a personal, pantheistic religious outlook:

> My attitude towards religious ideas is definitely influenced by going to Mexico. For each big festival, a different shrine is made. People go from home to home, visiting each other's shrine, placing objects on them, singing in front of them. There is a web of connections between the shrines in the neighbourhood.[10]

Inspired by these painted plywood and electric-light con-
structions, Neighbour made a couple of early versions of her
own. These include *Bouquet of Flowers* (1987) and *Gems* and
*Untitled* (both 1988). But it was the crown of thorns image
circling the rose window at St. Ines Church that was to significantly influence the artist. Neighbour began to make lith-
ographs featuring the crown of thorns. The braided circular
image eventually mutated into wreaths, in what she calls a
"degraded crown of thorns configuration." *Trance Wreath*
(1988) was a turning point:

> It wasn't figurative. It didn't have any concrete references. It did
> have the braided crown of thorns configuration, but there were
> no thorns on it – it was just this huge, oval shaped braid with
> all these lights on it. And when I finally fired the thing up – it
> had about a hundred lights on it – they were blinking on and
> off in random sequences. I hung the thing up on the wall and
> thought, well now I'm finally getting somewhere.[11]

The crown of thorns was the basic form behind a series of
images that included several types of crowns, floral wreaths
and abstract curvilinear weaves. It is possible to see in the
crown of thorns a formal relationship with other circular
curving forms like the Mobius strip or the ourabourous, the
snake eating its tail as an ancient symbol of all-consuming
time. The adaptations of the crown of thorns made by
Neighbour followed the anagogical tradition of the icon,
turning the symbol of torture into a mystical symbol of victory (the wreath) and imperial authority (the crown) and an
object of meditation (mandala).

While she would work on a crown image in print,
Neighbour would create a corresponding light work. During
an artist's residency in Toronto's artist-run print shop Open
Studio in 1989 she created the large *Black Wreath* (1990), a
painted plywood and electric light construction. Similarly, the

linoleum-cut *Crown of the Kingdom of Bavaria*, of 1989, was followed by its painted plywood cognate *Crown*, of 1991.

Neighbour was initially reluctant to show the light sculpture. "It was sort of in its formative stages and I was fooling around a bit and I wasn't showing it to anybody. It was a completely personal thing for me that was never intended to see the light of day."[12] It was as though she had trapped the genie in a bottle and feared taking the lid off. But she did venture to show *Festival Wreath* together with *Black Wreath* at her Open Studio residency exhibition.[13] The contrast must have been striking. Exhibiting the two pieces together as much as said, "Here is the dark and angry work that I do in my day job as a printmaker, and here is the bright and colourful work I do at home for fun."

The artist's split personality was on full display in her exhibition "The Other Mind," 1991, at the Red Head Gallery in Toronto. One side of the gallery featured her print work and on the other side were installed the light works. "The Other Mind" was clearly divided into Lisa Neighbour's day job and her night job, her past and her future. *Festival Wreath*, *Trance Wreath*, *Crown* and *Lotus* were each exhibited opposite their corresponding prints. Searching for a way to bring it all together, Neighbour distanced herself from the objects and speculated on more esoteric motivations. "Each idea is part of a map or sign post, directing me to a state of mind where I can rest and create. My work is tangible evidence and a record of this search."[14]

Nevertheless, the genie had been let out of the bottle. Neighbour was showing a body of work that was personal and not part of any proscribed style or content. She was giving herself permission to deviate from the printmaking discipline in which she had been educated, and setting out on a new and uncharted course. A place had been found where she could "rest and create," and the fact that it didn't much look like anything else being exhibited at the time left her without the signposts of familiar art language. Although she received much support and encouragement to pursue the light-sculpture work, there was no one to contextualize or interpret it. She was on her own, and in that isolation, she was looking to other voices and other ways of thinking to make sense of it all:

> I was looking for some way to connect them up. I was doing some research into how other people were defining similar experiences using the symbolism of light and darkness to describe philosophical and religious concepts which are hard to describe. It is interesting to see that a completely different culture was talking about things in a way that I could really understand.[15]

In 1992, Neighbour collaborated with Carlo Cesta and the art collaborators Fastwurms for the Toronto Sculpture Garden installation *Artes Moriendi*. Three distinct sculptures created an installation that commented on death, ecology and the failures of modernism, by imaginatively recasting the sculpture garden as part of neighbouring St. James Cathedral's missing graveyard. Despite the group effort, Neighbour's work stood apart from the other two installations. While Cesta and Fastwurms played with the ironies of historical mausoleum and sepulchre architecture in the modernist style, Neighbour contributed a three-dimensional abstract swirl of light that continued her interest in the crown motif – a three-dimensional *Trance Wreath*. In the context of funerary monuments it became a sort of electrified mortal coil. Dai Skuse perceived the developing mystical metaphorical core to Neighbour's work:

> Christian mysticism meets folk art futurism. Images of rose window cathedrals and spiral galaxies, crowns of thorns and satellite gyroscopes collide in the simplicity and sincere presentation of outsider art. At the centre of Neighbour's sphere and the heart of the memorial's equation, death is a metaphor of spirit and flight, a construction about the yearning to escape

from gravity and the burdens of the body, and to move freely within the music of the heavenly spheres.[16]

The light sculpture may have been effective in the Red Head Gallery in 1991, but the work was spectacular outside at night. In the dark, the work became a set piece – an installation. And the parallels of exhibiting art in the dark–the spectacles of the movie theatre, the fun house and the night presentation of commercial signage of city streets – are all aspects of pop-cultural "futurism" and electrification that contextualize the work. The contrast of ambient darkness with the illuminated works brought mysticism into the discussion: the metaphorical opposition of clarity and obscurity, enlightenment and blindness – symbols of knowledge, ignorance, hope and fear. These symbols have long been part of western culture and in some very real way were part of our lives in the early 1990s.

Neighbour's 1993 exhibition, "In the Dark," consisted of thirteen small plywood paintings, each punctuated by a single light bulb or string of lights. The works were named for various levels of divination, a realm of esoteric knowledge in which Neighbour had recently become interested.[17] Wired one to the next, they formed a daisy chain of points of coloured light in an otherwise darkened space. The centralized circular form that began with the influence of the rose window crown-of-thorns motif, that continued in the *Trance Wreath* and *Lotus* works of her first Red Head show, and that appeared most recently in the *Artes Moriendi* work, continued here in the form of floral, oval, circular and lozenge shapes.

"In the Dark" was first and foremost an installation. The individual pieces were simplified in favour of a total ambient presence – most of the works in the show having only a single electrical bulb. In this installation, Neighbour was moving closer to her original experience of Portuguese festival decoration, where the individual iconic objects more than made up for their lack of technical virtuosity by their vast array. The illuminated church standing in dialogue and contrast to the commercial lights of the city streets was an aspect of the festival decoration's charm. Moreover it was about light as a religious metaphor. High above the ground, the festival images were like constellations in the night sky, symbols of a benign and benevolent God.

"In the Dark," on the other hand, was an enclosed gallery. The spectator was surrounded by low-level-light-emitting objects. On the two end walls, sequenced strings of light bulbs in the works of *Astromancy* and *Oculomancy* created a flashing dialogue across the length of the gallery. Connected to them on the two long walls were twelve works that each featured a single bulb on a shaped coloured surface. The single centralized bulbs recalled mythical cyclopes – each icon of divination seemed to contain an omen within its dark contour shadow.

"In the Dark" was a painterly exercise in the use of volumes of light and dark for aesthetic effect, similar perhaps to the paintings of New York artist Ross Bleckner, where the existence of points of light makes the spectator more aware of the surrounding darkness. Light in this context was illumination withheld, like existence in a tunnel – a space where light was indeed a long way off:

> Up to this point, my work has documented a series of visual/emotional obsessions, not quite understood but deeply felt. In this exhibition, I am aware of the darkness in which I have been caught, but I am still in it, trying to analyze the experience. Instead of rushing ahead of myself, I am taking a good look at this obscure and formative place, trying to see its beauty before I move on.[18]

The cave of the cyclops, that Homeric symbol of irrational and arbitrary cruelty, was that "obscure and formative place" in which we were living in 1993.

By cunning and with luck, Ulysses and his surviving crew escaped from Polyphemus' cave. From the vantage of the current year, one can say that 1993's "inevitable and grimly certain apocalypse" was similarly averted, in the short term at least. Lisa Neighbour's art of darkness evolved from a meditation on the absence of light into apotropaic talismans and glowing objects of meditations and desire. "In the Dark" spawned *Eye on the Square*, Neighbour's 1994 installation of a monumental cyclopean eye on the Cambridge Public Library. And while *Eye on the Square* was directly derived from the earlier work *Oculomancy*, its installation outdoors high up on the side of the library building harkened back to the Portuguese festival decoration, the original inspiration for the light sculpture. Where *Oculomancy* was ominous, *Eye on the Square* was festive, one might even say celebratory. In the context of the library it became a combination humanistic icon and lucky amulet. The *Eye* also continued the mandala-like magnetism that all of the light sculpture seemed to possess. The centralized circular, or in this case, oval format, when combined with the electric lights, was transfixing and hypnotic.

Neighbour seemed to acknowledge the primary, hypnotic effect of her work in her press release for the exhibition "Luminous" at the Red Head in 1995:

> The exhibition is based on states of mind such as meditation and dreaming, which lead to a different perception of physical sensation and manifestation. During states of altered consciousness, the physical body may feel weightless, huge, small, invisible, made of light or made up of shadow. The environment appears as an intricate pattern, into which the dreamer fits without a seam. The absence of boundaries between self and environment may be frightening at times, but also a great relief from the restrictions of gender, age and location.

"Luminous" followed in the hypnotic lineage of *Lotus* and *Trance Wreath*, acquiring scale along the way from works like *Artes Moriendi* and *Eye on the Square*. All of these pieces

begged the question: was it the aesthetic object itself as sig-
nifier that commanded such intense response, or was it rather
the metaphor and the desire that this work signified? Was it
our age-old fascination with fire and its ersatz equivalent, the
filament bulb, or was it the promise that it symbolized? The
1996 exhibition "Loot" at the Koffler Gallery in Toronto and
the "Dalgas Underground" exhibition in Copenhagen of the
same year proposed the literal option: the object of aesthetic desire was a kind of pirate's treasure – a dream of vast
wealth or happiness or spiritual salvation – something at
once available and yet unattainable. The group exhibition
"Dalgas Underground" took place in a series of second-
world-war-era air-raid shelters.[19] In one of these concrete
bunkers, Neighbour installed a series of miners' lamps to
light a path strewn with coins. At the end of the trail of coins
was a small chest that was modeled and painted and adorned
with fake gems and gold-painted coins. The pot of gold, the
light at the end of the tunnel, was, of course, fake. The installation was a literal illustration of Neighbour's effort to take
"a good look at this obscure and formative place, trying to
see its beauty before I move on."

Lisa Neighbour did move on. While she has continued
to make sculpture with electric lights, the subject of her
work has begun to shift away from the metaphorical opposition of light and dark toward a deeper understanding of the
materials with which she is working. Circuitry, conductivity
and connectivity – fundamental principles of electricity –
have become her new metaphors and working models.
Emerging from her work with electrical wiring is an appreciation for the strange and mysterious power of electricity
and the web of connections that make it accessible. *Super
Power*, exhibited at the Red Head Gallery in 1997, is the first
example of Neighbour's stripped-down work. Sixty varied
table-top lamps – minus shades and outfitted with bulbs of
various shapes, sizes and colours – were wired to a single

source of power. Gone were the hand-painted and hand-shaped surfaces. Gone was the singular, centrally composed object. *Super Power* was the skeleton – the wiring, the light fixtures – of all of the previous works.

Neighbour's most recent works, *Why Knot?* Of 1998 and *The Breeze*, *Rope Lights* and *Hurricane Andrew* of 1999, have taken her further into the metaphorical association of circuitry, connectivity and patterns of energy. While light is still a feature of all these works, the electrical power is now being dispersed among a collection of small appliances. In *Why Knot?* And *The Breeze* she has rediscovered the much-maligned craft of macramé to decoratively braid the wiring for a loose assembly of clock radios, fans and lamps. In *Rope Lights*, Neighbour learned techniques of braiding and boondoggle to combine electrical cords into thick bundles. In *Hurricane Andrew*, she connected lights, fans and a heat lamp in what she calls an "electro-magnetic spiral," representing the elemental forces of waves of sound, air, light, and heat with familiar domestic machines.

Lisa Neighbour's light sculpture emerged from the very specific context of art and culture in Toronto in the second half of the 1980s and the first half of the 1990s. The cultural changes that took place during this time appear massive in retrospect. Quietly, Neighbour synthesized imagery, media, philosophical and religious texts and that intangible quality sometimes called *Zeitgeist*. Her body of work was the actualization of a personal quasi-religious mythology that embraced the hopes and fears that she harboured within and that were reflected back by her community of family, friends and colleagues. It may have been a coincidence that in a time of suffering, the crown of thorns – the Christian *Ecce Homo* symbol – became a motif of ongoing influence in her work. The braided circular icon transformed itself variously over the decade into regal crowns, wreaths, mandalas, gyroscopes and eyes. On a deeper, conceptual level the motif persisted into the circuitry itself and in the braided and macraméd electrical cords, and finally in the electromagnetic spiral of *Hurricane Andrew*. The braided spiral is a literal description of interconnection and continuity, metaphors of personal relationships and the life cycle that were important to believe in during a time of darkness. And during that time of darkness, Lisa Neighbour chose to work with light.

## Notes

1. From *Bullfinch's Mythology*, Chapter XXIX.

2. Oliver Girling, "The Coup: No Contest. Lisa Neighbour's show at the Red Head Gallery," *eye*, 30 December, 1993).

3. To get a sense of ecological awareness and alarm in the art community in the early 1990s, see Jocelyn Laurence, "Water, Earth & Air: Visions of Our Endangered Planet," *Canadian Art* (Winter, 1990).

4. See, among others, Lewis Lapham, "Sermons in Mixed Media," *Harper's* (May, 1993), pp. 4-5.

5. Ralph Rugoff, "Just Pathetic," (Los Angeles: Rosamund Felsen Gallery, 1990).

6. Adam Gopnik, "Death in Venice," *New Yorker* (2 August, 1993), pp. 67-73.

7. Author's interview with Lisa Neighbour, 31 March, 2000.

8. Carol Barbour, "Lisa Neighbour: What Do I Believe?" *Artworld* (Fall, 1993).

9. A parallel might be drawn with the Russian artists Kasimir Malevich, Wassily Kandinsky and Natalia Goncharova, who at the turn of the century developed an interest in folk art in reaction to the existing academic models.

10. Barbour, *op. cit.*

11. Interview.

12. *Ibid.*

13. "Recent Work" (Toronto: Open Studio Gallery, 1989).

14. "Lisa Neighbour: The Other Mind," press release, Red Head Gallery, Toronto, 28 June, 1991.

15. Interview. Neighbour's statement from "In the Dark" is also relevant: "Darkness and light are the archetypical symbols of Sufism because they are natural, immediate self-expressions of a root experience of the Divinity. Light and darkness are, for the Sufi, metaphorical experiences. Existence is light. When the Absolute

appears to the consciousness of the mystic, it appears as an uncontaminated unity, as light. All multiplicity disappears into darkness."
– from Laleh Bakhtiear, *SUFI: Expressions of the Mystic Quest* (London: Thames and Hudson, 1976), p. 91.

16. Dai Souse, *Arts Modern* (Toronto: The Toronto Sculpture Garden, 1992).

17. The artists provided the following legend with the press release:

Crystalomancy: gazing into a crystal ball to divine the future.

Ylomancy: tossing sticks or twigs, observing fallen branches and reading signs.

Psychomancy: intuition and psychic powers.

Arithmancy: the study of numbers and their patterns, to predict the future.

Bibliomancy: reading random passages from books and interpreting their predictions.

Cephalomancy: dissection of animal or human brains for clues to upcoming events.

Cyclomancy: the use of a revolving device to reveal numbers, letters or symbols.

Aeromancy: observation of the atmospheric conditions for portents of the future.

Oculomancy: examination of a person's eyes to determine their future.

Botanomancy: observing the growth of plants and seeds to foresee future events.

Anthropomancy: the dissection and examination of the entrails of human and animal sacrifices.

Ornithomancy: reading the behaviour and appearance of birds.

Pyromancy: looking for omens in the burning of various materials, sacred fires and candles.

Astromancy: divination by the movements of the moon and planets, an early form of astrology.

From Lisa Neighbour, "In the Dark," press release, Red Head Gallery, Toronto, 16 May, 1993.

18. Lisa Neighbour, "In the Dark," artist's statement, Red Head Gallery, Toronto, 1993.

19. In Toronto, the Nether Mind collective had been exhibiting in the dark, dank basements of old factory buildings since 1991.

# Ego, Power,
# and Urban Reality
# in Canadian Literature

## Brian L. Flack

Whenever I think about the "aesthetic" of Canadian writing, I fall victim to a peculiar swooning and remain in that state for some time. The word itself inflates to unmanageable proportions and blank, bitter, prairie landscapes begin to haunt my dreams. In an effort to overcome this, I retrace my steps from graduate school. I reread bits and pieces of a few of the so-called seminal "aesthetic" texts (Frye, Atwood, Mandel, etc.); recall best forgotten, because they were very nearly unintelligible, lectures on the subject; and still find myself roaming in a lethal wilderness, feeling both intellectually impotent and curiously disturbed.

Why, I keep asking myself, do none of the "nice," old theories appear to apply anymore? Why do they not reflect my feeling regarding the ethic, or direction, or explanation, or whatever it is I am looking for, of Canadian writing today? Why does it seem that something is unraveling here that, in many respects, defies our age-old, mainstream historical analysis? Why, I am finally forced to conclude, do I persist in looking to the past – to theories already shopworn – for an answer?

Nothing I can put my finger on satisfies me because I realize it is necessary to define, maybe even to create, some new analytical model, one that talks about where we are in terms of where we are going or what we are trying to accomplish, but not in terms solely focused on where we have come from!

The principal problem is that we have gotten into the habit of discussing our own literature rooted, perhaps even buried, in the excesses of the past and that strikes me as both short-sighted and inviting of narrow, historical rather than imaginative, progressive approaches to current Canadian fiction and poetry.

To clarify this point, let me digress some years, to the mid-nineteenth century, and quote from Thomas De Quincey, from his *Letters to a Young Man*.

> Books, we are told, propose to instruct or amuse. Indeed! . . . The true antithesis to knowledge in this case is not pleasure but power. All that is literature seeks to communicate power. All that is not literature to communicate knowledge.[1]

Now, that is a statement to inflame even the meekest among us, but in this inflammation must we not ultimately agree with its essential truthfulness, for once angered or inflamed are we not in a position either to exert or demonstrate our power? I believe that De Quincey came as close as anyone has to putting some substantial flesh on the question of what makes literature: what makes it important in the beginning, what makes it enduring, and what is instructive about it.

The creative imagination translated by a self-conscious artist through the innovative use of language into a demonstration of power is what some Canadian writers are on the verge of accomplishing in the twenty-first century, and this has been, I am sorry to say, without either the wholesale encouragement or even the blessing of the publishing industry or the public. For too long we have wallowed in a self-satisfied stupor characterized by a witless appreciation of a tradition that cannot be made consistent with the "power" concept suggested by De Quincey. Basically, we ceaselessly and repetitively examine our pioneer heritage believing that familiarity with its static state of mind will salvage a national literature for us. For much too long we have persisted in teaching our students that the pious backwoodsman, the man and woman dominated by the land and God – and their exercises of power – are the keys to what we are and what we will become.

But this has been a costly error, so costly that there is much evidence in this country today to suggest that what De Quincey was pillorying 150 years ago is still the prevailing opinion. "To instruct or amuse," and all-too-often the latter, is the common, current perception of what literature is intended to do, whereas the communication of power, both the writer's and the reader's, and by inference the nation's, is what's at stake! And until we recognize the importance of this simple axiom to the process of writing and then reading, I maintain it is just not possible to have a literature that is particularly meaningful or enduring, or perhaps even worthwhile because it does not reflect either the circumstances or the values of the present-day urban realities of Canada.

Let me embellish this thought with a short but startlingly horrific example of how ignorant the literary establishment is of the fairly recent emergence in Canada of an ego/power/urban-based literature. It is a personal account and I think that even as an isolated incident it speaks eloquently of the extent of the problem we face at the moment. Not long ago, I received a letter from one publishing house that contained a statement which is a prime example of the malaise I have just identified.

Some astute editor, forever vigilant to the winds of change that are most certainly blowing, began his or her reply thus: "The primary purpose of fiction is to entertain: not to set forth questions and try to answer them." Not entirely unsympathetic to the psychological damage that can be done by embarrassment, I will decline to identify the publisher, although God knows I ought to scream the name from a high building, merely as a precautionary warning to other unsuspecting writers.

The phrase that most puzzled and disturbed me was "the primary purpose of fiction is to entertain." The more I tried to believe that an editor of a respected house – renowned for its literary fiction – had not uttered this irresponsible unthinking, narrow-minded, wrong-headed (even in historical terms) phrase, the more it infuriated me. The motives that prompted this rather arbitrary assessment of the function of literature are far too ensconced in this country and, unless they are squarely addressed, the purveyors of such an attitude threaten to bury all of us.

But before I tackle the question of what is happening here, I would like to spend a few moments assessing what exactly this statement reveals. Or, more importantly, what editorial myopia it conceals. And suggest that it elevates De Quincey's assertion to the level of one almost prophetic in its implications.

This editor was advocating "amusement," as De Quincey would have it, to promote the idea that the reader's fancy must be tickled so that he or she might come away from the experience of reading with a "good" feeling. It is this attitude which lies behind the general and somewhat incomprehensible public acceptance, public reverence, of a book like WP Consciously's *Shoeless Joe*, to fall upon an obvious, but by no means singular, example of the sort of writing that irks me. I could have settled on others that rely on a stereotyped, romantic vision of life – almost anything by Alice Monro or Margaret Atwood, or even the Salem novels of Matt Cohen (in fairness, he does break out of the mold in other novels like *Johnny Crackle Sings* or *Korsoniloff*, or *The Spanish Doctor*) – but Consciously will do.

*Shoeless Joe* is a "nice" book. It has a "nice" protagonist, virtuous to a fault. It has a "nice" heroine, a little lady who stays at home and supports her man in typical, traditional weak-minded fashion. It has a "nice" child, a "nice" dog, even a "nice" reclusive writer who trots out, on cue, in a rather "nice" way. The only non-niceness is embedded in a few of the "nice" wife's relatives and they haven't got a chance from the outset, so half-heartedly evil (perhaps to be read as "real") are they. The book is flattering to its hero in every imaginable way and hardly thought-provoking at all.

In effect, if this book is examined outside Conscious-ly's other work, which for the most part is powerful and controlled, it is a tribute to a demonstrably egoless author. And because of this it's boring, boring, boring. "Nicely" written, soft of language, possessing the odd gossamer-like rural image, but boring. Where, I ask, is the author's power flexed? Over his subject? No! Over his hero? No! Over his audience? Again no! Unless glazed eyes are a sign of this dominance. Plainly, power is not there in any form. But, nonetheless, *Shoeless Joe* has been judged a "good" book and everyone loved it, except perhaps me. It won't last, I predict, the film, *Field of Dreams,* notwithstanding, without serious criticism. Why? Because it doesn't exhibit any character or strength as defined by the author's exercise of power, not to mention anything of a national character given that it was written by an American, about Americans, about an American pastime, for Americans. Perhaps that's why it was a Canadian best-seller and generally adored.

The key to a power-based Canadian literature of the future lies elsewhere. It rests with the emergence and refinement of the urban ego, both the writer's and the reader's, working as complements to each other. And there are several excellent examples of this which I will get to shortly.

But first, how should the ego function in the creative process? Consider for a moment, this passage from one of Italo Calvino's novels, *If on a Winter's Night a Traveller*, wherein the narrator contemplates his own role in the narrative.

I am not the sort of person who attracts attention, I am an anonymous presence against an even more anonymous background. If you, reader, couldn't help picking me out among the people getting off the train and continued following me in my to- and fro-ing between bar and telephone, this is simply because I am called "I" and this is the only thing you know about me, but this alone is reason enough for you to invest a part of yourself in the stranger "I". Just as the author, since he has no intention of telling about himself, decided to call the character "I" as if to conceal him, not having to name or describe him, because any other name or attribute would define him more than this stark pronoun; still, by the very fact of writing "I" the author feels driven to put into this "I" a bit of himself of what he feels or imagines he feels.[2]

With this "confession," so to speak, in mind, I would like to say that I believe there are potentially three uses the writer can make of his ego, his "I." He can suppress it. He can disguise it. Or, he can give it free rein. The first two breed amusement, perhaps even contribute to what De Quincey called the communication of knowledge. The latter choice, in effect, evolves, over the course of a novel or poem or short story, into a demonstration of raw, authorial power and, since the ego is the executive of the personality, it controls this demonstration. Further, since it is the ego which faces reality, or that which exists, head-on, the writer's notions of power – his personal conception of its creation, use and demise – which define the individual's mastery over, or contentment with, or loathing of that which is, become of supreme and lasting importance. They make a work. They make it reach out to an audience, take its members by the hand, lead them into new and foreign places, and treat them to the experience called real life, for better or worse. But the writer who lacks this control, who fails to recognize and utilize his "power principle," cannot do this. He can entertain, amuse, kindle fleeting excitement, even communicate knowledge if he is particularly skillful, but he cannot communicate power which is the bedrock of a true and enduring literature.

Canadian writers, by and large, are only just learning to exercise this power. Some are doing it well, others poorly, but those who are doing it are in the forefront of a movement which, I suggest, will shortly (if this is not already so) define our cumulative experience as a people. We are in the process of a transition that will be marked by our literary development from a rurally defined, powerless culture (in our own minds, that is) to an urban one that exerts power rather than suffers from its effects willingly, almost as a penance, but with conviction, under the thumb of nature, where thin pleasures and little else are despairingly clutched at often without thought or caution.

Certainly this, then, goes some way toward explaining why I have so much trouble with the word "aesthetics." For my purposes, as a Canadian, a writer, and, hopefully, an innovator, the term is generalist when we have to be more specific. Studying concepts and theories of what is beautiful and tasteful is not and never will be futile, quite the contrary. Such endeavours are illuminating and often pleasurable, but systems of rules and principles are no more than encouragements to embrace limiting factors and characterize stiff, frequently outdated ways of relating to that which exists now, to that which is in the process of evolving. To approach a work seeking some sense of its aesthetic value and nothing else is to use the past to interpret the present, and the time for such short-sightedness has to give way if we are to move into the future with a distinct and progressive impression of our own self-worth, as writers on the one hand and as a nation of individuals on the other.

I propose that we look at what is happening, and has been for many years in the work of some writers, in a new and radically different light, in terms of the creative process and in relation to what is or exists, not in relation to what was. As a template for the present state of affairs vis-a-vis what we are becoming, not as an explanation or rationale for the present as a creation solely of the past. And entwined inextricably with this conception is the exercise or communication of power: the writer's as it stimulates the reader's. Ultimately a recognition of what De Quincey claimed constituted a true literature.

What, then, does this way of thinking impart to the use that is made of the written word? First, it demands a writer who is always keenly aware of his or her own presence in what is being created, an artist whose ego is given free rein, as I pointed out before; one whose ego, once given this freedom, becomes, to a greater or lesser degree, the object of the discussion or narrative that defines the work of art. This constitutes an exertion of power, the writer's, and invites by it the reader to exert an equal but reflexive form of power which is his or her active examination and judgement of the writer's bared self. And how is this accomplished? In two ways:

> by urging, even demanding, the reader to investigate, as the work unfolds, the process that reveals it; and by making the vehicle which gives form to the work – language – an element of equal importance to the intent of the narrative line itself.

Further, it is my belief that this transition in the process of writing – which might be described as a shift from the objective to the subjective – goes hand in hand with an increase in the incidence of truly urban novels, stories and poems. This need not necessarily be the case, but I have found few urban Canadian novels that fail to rely, to some extent, on this meticulous examination of the creative process which is ultimately the study of the individual's struggle to cope with a mechanized, impersonal world that threatens, daily, to obliterate any sense of that individual. In other words, it is necessary to push back as hard, or harder, than you are pushed.

Because I believe writers are coming, in a trickle, to an embracing of this inevitability, it does not surprise me to find novelists and short story writers like Hugh Garner (*Cabbagetown*, which appeared in the early 1950s); or Seymour Blicker (*Schmucks*, which appeared in the early 1970s); or David Lewis Stein (*City Boys*, which appeared in the mid 1970s), or D.M. Fraser (*The Voice of Emma Sachs*, which appeared in the early 1980s); or Michael *Ondaatje* (*In the Skin of a Lion*, which appeared in the late 1980s); or Douglas Coupland (*Generation X*, which appeared in the early 1990s). Or poets like Al Purdy who, in the years before his death, became ever more hard-edged and conscious of the power he could extract from and bring to bear against his vision, or John Newlove or George Bowering or Tom Wayman or Andrew Wreggitt. Even an overlooked fellow like Crad Kilodney, Toronto's "street-writer-salesman," pilloried for his serious stylistic shortcomings by the conventionally literary, has much to tell us about the study of self and power in urban Canadian writing.

None of the writers I have just alluded to are strictly autobiographical in their approach (a dangerous side-effect to self-immersion in a work). That is, you cannot trace people or incidents directly back to the author's experience (with the odd exception, particularly among the poets), but for the most part, as D. M. Fraser so aptly put it:

> Imagined events occur in the brief lives of imaginary people, in a world which bears at most an approximate, superficial and largely coincidental resemblance to the one in which we actually live.[3]

To widen our base in this examination, I believe we can draw some comparable and favourable lessons from the situation that existed in America in the late 1940s and 1950s, perhaps even into the 1960s. A loosely knit group of individuals whom we now call, collectively, the "Beats" issued in their work and by the example of their lives, a challenge to the literary establishment. "We are power!" they seemed to be saying. "We represent it! We revel in it! We are both the victims and the masters of it! It is our life force!" They turned the creative process inside out, made it as important, perhaps more so, than the message. Here, perhaps, it is important to note that it was Marshall McLuhan, a Canadian, who told us years ago that the medium was the message.

They made out of language a laboratory where experimentation in an urban milieu became high art, and they forced readers to become one with them on their geographical and intellectual jaunts. No longer would receptive passivity on the readers' part be acceptable. Their presence was required in the car, or on the street, or in the cafe. "I" became, for the first time in American writing, the dominant pronoun. "How are we to live?" a chant that accompanied their quest. These writers examined themselves and their experiences brazenly, against the backdrop of urban America, which they saw as either oppressive or repressive depending on their point of view, with only cursory disguising of reality or their involvement in it. Even a writer as perceptive as Norman Mailer, in his controversial essay of 1957, "The White Negro," said of the ethic that lay behind this phenomenon: "Know Thyself and Be Thyself."[4]

Names and addresses were omitted from their fiction, it seemed, only to save the principals from what would have amounted to destructive public attention, and even then they were not particularly successful in saving some of their company. And that was fiction! The poets named names and told secrets. Theirs was a creative revolution, a reality uncontested by literary historians and readers alike.

Writers have always examined their innermost thoughts

and feelings and translated them into themes they wrote. But
the exercise of power as practiced by the "Beats," became a
primary factor in the distillation of experience; the fictional
veneer grew thinner and, in modern terms at least, the city,
their home, took on the role of temple – as once the wood-
land copse had – and the writers cast themselves as leading
actors and demanded that their readers fill the roles of supporting actors.

In America, this kind of indulgence became the catch-
word of a generation. Their methods of inculcating this belief
– this way of life – ranged from relative sobriety in John
Clellon Holmes' *Go* to the hectic testimonies of Jack
Kerouac in *On the Road*, where characters' actions, ideas, or
what have you reflected the fact they were "mad to live, mad
to talk, mad to be saved, desirous of everything at the same
time . . ."[5] Self-destructive? Yes! Disorderly? Yes! Passionate?
Yes! Decadent? Yes! Emblematic of the distortions of self-
consciousness? Yes! But they were at all times power-seeking
too, power-obsessed, power-hungry, noble characters in their
noble city possessed of noble objectives: self-examination,
self-actualization.

Consider, for example, how Clellon Holmes' *Go* begins:

> Last week I got the idea that the one aim of my intercourse
> with other people is to prevent them from noticing how brit-
> tle and will-less I have become.[6]

The narrative that follows details the quest of Clellon
Holmes' persona, Paul Hobbes, to reverse that perception by
a reckless immersion in life. Or Allen Ginsberg's poem "My
Alba." It begins:

> Now that I've wasted
> Five years in Manhattan
> life decaying
> talent a blank

and ends:

> dawn breaks it's only the sun
> the East smokes O my bedroom
> I am damned to Hell what
> Alarmclock is ringing.[7]

It is his recognition of the need for both control and release. Gregory Corso, for that matter, wrote a poem in 1958 that he called "Power," so near to the surface of his being was the realization that dominance over anything seen as oppressive was not only desired but necessary.

So here we are in Canada about fifty years after this incredible alteration in literary motivation in America and signs that our own revolution is underway are beginning to be seen and felt. It is not "Beat" by any stretch of the imagination, but it has the potential to reform many of our opinions, as both writers and readers, regarding what makes literature and consequently will have a considerable effect on the type of book that will come to dominate our experience. Those who identify with this change can call themselves anything they want, but certainly some years hence the ascent to an urban literary preoccupation with an emphasis on the examination of and experimentation with personal power and the self will be recognized as a turning point in our fiction and poetry.

I have no wish to be restrictive and cloud the issue by suggesting there was a specific beginning to this movement, but I will point to Leonard Cohen's *The Favourite Game* of 1963 as perhaps the herald that Canadian literature as entertainment alone was in serious trouble. Cohen gave notice that the city we were in the process of growing up with was a place where nothing happened and demanded, by so doing, that this must change. Subsequently, in *Beautiful Losers*, he records the nature of that change as the old man at the end transforms himself into a movie of Ray Charles. A man in the process of becoming his own movie is a graphic image of his assertion of power over a seemingly all-powerful, mechanical universe, a demonstration that the "I," the outcast "I," can triumph over the structures of the past which are sterile and death-oriented with an emphasis on external obedience rather than on internal self-reliance. In a way this transformation of the body is violent and necessarily so. It is emblematic of a kind of suicide and rebirth.

Violence and power are compatriots, blood relations, and for this vision to be effected without compromise or delay, violence in the exercise of power is demanded. Jack Kerouac and Neal Cassady wrecked cars and property. Allen Ginsberg wrecked long-standing notions of the "aesthetics" of poetry and screeched in "Howl" that because of these relics he had seen "the best minds of [his] generation destroyed by madness."[8] Cohen's Breavman directs the violence towards himself and is, in the process, liberated. He is, as far as I'm concerned, the first true symbol in Canadian fiction of the self's victory over its oppressors by the exertion of inner power unencumbered by either restrictive spiritualism or duty – the self's transcendence for the sake of the self, the first symbol of the creative wonderland that exists within the urban environment which must inevitably become the vehicle we use to define ourselves.

Power, the exertion of it, dispels doubt. Those who recognize this are becoming more assertive in their writing, less reactive. Some writers are no longer afraid to cast blame or insult if need be. Nor are they fearful of their own failures and victories. And they have finally realized that this must be done in a language and form that celebrates what is, the actual, human experience. And the only way to achieve this is to demonstrate our control over or mastery of the actuality which is modern urban life.

William Carlos Williams, in his poem "Paterson" said,

> A man like a city
>
> But
>
> only one man – like a city. [9]

Thomas De Quincey advised anyone who would listen that, "All that is literature seeks to communicate power." John Newlove, in a poem called "I Talk To You," asked,

> To whom shall I talk except
> my exhaustive self ? [10]

Gwen MacEwan, in her "Poem I Improvised Around A First Line," lamented,

> O baby, what Hell to be Greek in this country –
> And in without wings but burning anyway. [11]

In my novel, *In Seed Time*, I said, hoping to find something justifiable in the destruction of time-worn dependencies on the past:

> The point, I suppose, is to be aware of Time. I can't help feeling smothered by it though. The days pass but they do not change. Nothing changes anymore, for change has been outlived. [12]

Furthermore, in another novel, *With A Sudden & Terrible Clarity*, counter-pointing the hope for the future with the death of the past, I had a small boy act out his frustration standing beside his father's grave. Of his own embryonic assertions of power repulsed by an ignorant, close-minded authority, the adult, I wrote:

> His future had crumbled as he stood in their midst begging for the truth, but he had been forced to digest the falsehoods offered by fearful, dishonest people. He had been repulsed by their black jackets, ties, pants and dresses. Black veils obscured what might have been telltale signs of truth reflected in the

women's eyes. And the blackness of the expressions he did see confused him more.[13]

That paragraph is descriptive, in many respects, of the crisis that exists in Canadian writing. Truth versus falsehood is essentially the same conflict as that which I have elsewhere alluded to as power versus passivity. Truth and power breed self-realization and a sense of well-being in the individual. They are representative of a world where the "I," the writer and even the reader to some degree, has control over his or her immediate environment and future, over the thoughts percolating in his or her own mind. Falsehood and passivity mark a world that is neither progressive nor nurturing of self-awareness, one that is destructive for the individual.

It seems to me that writers, artists, have to make a conscious choice between the two. They can opt for De Quincey's vision of a literature-free world, perhaps gain some knowledge, but it will be of the dubious sort characterized by receptivity not activity, or they can embrace his literary world – as the "Beats" did, as those Canadians I have mentioned are, as others in many cultures have – and exert their power through honesty and self-examination. I doubt a compromise scenario exists. If it does, I cannot imagine what it would be.

Canadians must not tolerate a fear of themselves, and by inference life, any longer. Cohen's Breavman (*The Favorite Game*) refused to do so and in order for him to accomplish this Cohen infused him with the burning flame of his own sense of power, his own need and the tools to penetrate his surface self so that he might discover what lay dormant beneath, buried, out of sight, but by no means impotent once unleashed. Douglas Coupland accomplished something of the same end in *Generation X*. His characters, alienated and seemingly without clear options in the repressive world handed down to them, imagine how they might abandon the dictates of the past, how they might achieve escape velocity. With a colourful tenacity, not to mention humour, they do break the patterns of the past, manage to look into their own hearts and souls, pass judgement on what they find wanting, and assert themselves. As one character muses:

> This is what I want: I want to lie on the razory brain-shaped rocks of Baja. I want to lie on these rocks with no plants around me, traces of brine on my fingers and a chemical sun burning up in the heaven. I would sacrifice anything to be given this offering.[14]

Both novels are expressions, I believe, of what De Quincey was hoping to pass on to future generations of writers: the means and the inspiration to seek out ways to unharness this power of the self. And because Canadians are fortunate to have the experiences of the American "Beats," for instance, to inform their wanderings and experimentations, they have little excuse for not heeding his message or their example.

Our task has already been defined. It is simply to make the creative process, as Joyce did, the single most important aspect of artistic endeavour and to assure our eventual success by adopting a certain self-consciousness toward our experience, by rendering the language we use reflective of actuality or real life, urban life. It will be no mean feat to achieve this end and those of us who subscribe to our need for a change in consciousness on a large scale will fail as often as we succeed until we are in complete control of ourselves and the means by which we make ourselves accessible to those who would emulate or look to us for a detailed philosophy of existence.

I do not want to imply, if I have done so, that this is a narrow, vainly channelled enterprise. It is not. What, after all, is more given to notions of multiplicity than the self? Schizophrenia is not necessarily a bad thing in a writer, I think, and the possibilities open to a true literary schizophrenic are limitless. The current urban reality is one rooted in scattered points of reference and it will take a self-conscious student of this system to dominate the system, to educate those victimized by it, those who are consistently undermined by the political and social turbulence of our times. In this respect it is important to note that even the suffering victim is capable of exercising power, power through self-awareness.

As I have already suggested, Leonard Cohen proclaimed the arrival of the future in *Beautiful Losers*. As the old man transformed himself into a movie of Ray Charles, a New Jew cried: "Hey. Somebody's making it!"[15] That people should realize this is possible is crucial. If one individual can do it others can follow by breaking ground for themselves. And it is up to today's writers to spread the word that the opportunity to "make it" exists and must be sustained.

Power over subject, method and self will do it. It may well be the only hope for survival in the midst of a limitless, mechanical, urban reality that constantly threatens to extinguish the tenuous hold the individual maintains. Writers need to demand some concrete reaction, some involvement, from readers and urge them to become actively involved in the creative process that is their own life. Force them to see authority for what it is and they will respond appreciatively and with considerable energy. Power is derived from energy. That is a basic tenet of science. It is the stuff from which great and lasting literature issues also.

## Notes

1. Thomas De Quincey, "Letters To A Young Man," in David Masson, ed., *The Collected Works of Thomas De Quincey: Volume X* (London: A & C Black, 1897), pp. 47-48.

2. Italo Calvino, *If on a Winter's Night a Traveller* (Toronto: Lester & Orpen Dennys Ltd, 1979), pp. 14-15.

3. D. M. Fraser, *The Voice of Emma Sachs* (Vancouver: Arsenal Editions,1982), p. 135.

4. Norman Mailer, "The White Negro," in Ann Charters, ed., *The Portable Beat Reader* (New York: Penguin Books, 1992), p. 601.

5. Jack Kerouac, *On the Road* (New York: Signet Books, 1957), p. 9.

6. Clellon Homes, *Go* (New York: Ace Books, 1957).

7. Allen Ginsberg, *Collected Poems: 1947-1980* (New York: Harper & Row, 1984), p. 89.

8. *Ibid.*, p. 126.

9. William Carlos Williams, *Paterson* (New York: New Directions, 1963), p. 15.

10. John Newlove, *Moving in Alone* (B.C.: Oolichan Books, 1977), p. 73.

11. Gwendolyn MacEwan, *Magic Animals: The Selected Poetry of Gwendolyn MacEwan* (Toronto: General Publishing Co., 1984), p. 40.

12. Brian Flack, *In Seed Time* (Cobalt: Highway Book Shop, 1978), 1.

13. Brian Flack, *With A Sudden & Terrible Clarity* (Windsor: Black Moss, 1985), p. 206.

14. Douglas Coupland, *Generation X* (New York: St. Martin's Press, 1991), p. 173.

15. Leonard Cohen, *Beautiful Losers* (New York: The Viking Press, 1966), p. 242.

# Social and Political Studies

# Dangerous Knowledge

Canadian Workers' Education

in the Decades of Discord

## Michael R. Welton

Labour history is a thriving academic enterprise in Canada; the study of workers' education is not. Nonetheless, adult educational historians are turning some attention to recovering the educational dimensions of workers' culture and politics,[1] and several prominent labour historians[2] have, in focusing on workers' attempts to create an oppositional culture, opened up important questions. How do workers in particular times and places come to understand themselves, their work, social institutions and competing ideologies? How do they acquire a set of competencies? How do they not only adapt to, but act transformingly in, societies presenting formidable barriers to autonomous workers' education? When we examine processes of industrial conflict and change through the learning lens, we can see that the battles are always intellectual and practical. Particular forms of social and political action proceed from an idea that alternatives to capitalism are necessary and possible. Before persons can change their behaviour and their society, they must first be enlightened as to that possibility. Collective enlightenment (the transformation of collective self-understanding and identity) is the learning catalyst, empowering actors to engage in, within limits, transformative action in the world. The struggles of workers in the turbulent decades under scrutiny can be viewed as a contest between supporters of conflicting visions of what constitutes valid enlightenment, empowerment, and transformative action. Thus, given the importance of ideas in generating action, and the importance of education in the creation and promotion of these ideas, education must always be considered in attempts to understand the larger processes of social conflict and change.[3] To understand and perhaps explain the wonderful complexities of workers' education, we need to situate workers' education in multiple contexts and discursive fields, examine the sites workers create for reflection (the organization of enlightenment), the critical themes they examine, and the outcomes of learning processes (the organization of action).

There are notorious difficulties in delineating the boundaries of workers' education. For my purposes, the boundaries ought to be drawn such that we can study both the "schools of labour" and "labour's schools." Simply defined, the schools of labour are the socially organized work places, embedded in networks of economic, social, and political control. Important technical, social, political and ideological experiential learning is occurring in the work place (which Marx called the "harsh but hardening school of labour"), and perhaps the strike is the important learning occasion directly linked to the work site. Labour's schools are those spaces workers themselves, their leaders or sympathetic pedagogues open up for reflection on the meaning of their work and culture. Labour's schools take many forms: (a) "educational movements" woven into particular social practices such as the assembly meeting (the Knights of Labour saw these as "schools of instruction") or political party activity; (b) specific educational forms created by the workers themselves (journals, newspapers, forums, and so on); and (c) educational forms provided for workers by agencies and institutions outside the workers' own organizations (Workers' Educational Association [WEA] and university extension programs).

In this essay, I am particularly interested in what I take to be a rather fascinating puzzle. In our ordinary language use in the field of adult education, we do, indeed, distinguish adult from workers' education (and wonder about some of the issues at the interface), and often talk about the emergence of "adult education" in, say, the 1920s.[4] There are several ways of understanding this. While adult learning is present at all times and places, we must reject the idea that "adult education" has an essence that only need be represented in appropriate, value-neutral scientific language. Adult education repeatedly resists paradigmatic control, slipping and sliding out of the professional educator's scientific grasp. Like the creature in Arnold Schwarzenegger's film, *The Predator*, it blends with the environment at times and then, when threatened, becomes visible, embodied. Likewise, adult education becomes visible and embodied only when it is constituted by a "discursive field" (ideas, texts, theories, use of language). But this constituting process is not a unitary, totalizing act. Competing discourses jostle and struggle over the control of the constituting process. In unsettling times of historical transition (Canada from the late nineteenth to the early twentieth century was shifting to a monopoly form of capitalist production and relations, just as late twentieth and early twenty-first century Canada is being transformed by the forces of global capitalism), oppositional forms of adult learning erupt in a multiplicity of sites precipitating the struggle to constitute "adult education."

Kathleen Rockhill's work on the professional construction of adult education in the U.S.A. suggests that "adult education" as a professional practice was constructed quite consciously to exclude socialism (viewed as dangerous knowledge), and she details the set of ideological constructs used to perform this task.[5] The professional "discursive field" wins out in the U.S.A. This, however, only subjugates alternative knowledge forms, casting them outside the arbitrarily delineated field. Still, they hover at the edges of the field, waiting for their time.

Discursive practices are, of course, related in complex ways to nondiscursive practices (social systems, class and gender divisions, economic needs, governmental institutions). Particular discursive practices are intimately bound up with social power and control. Knowledge/power, Foucault has taught us, cannot be thought apart.[6] This insight demands that we pay attention to the way adult education discourse sets the limits on what counts as authentic educational practice, and perhaps more important, social and political action. Adult education discourses might be read as a very important way that our society organizes its power relations.

My strategy in this examination of working class culture, from 1896 to 1922 is, first, to characterize the political economy and the labour movement's sense of collective identity, and then to examine the educational thought and initiatives occurring within the workers' movement as well as agencies outside the movement itself. As noted, the focus will be on the competing discursive fields vying for hegemony and control of the field. My conclusion is that some adult educators have, as one of their jobs, the quelling of the insurrections of subjugated knowledges. Others, it seems, have the task of participating in the insurrection itself.

## Working Class Culture: 1896-1922

From the late nineteenth century until the end of the World War I, Canada was a nation being transformed. As the monopoly form of capitalism emerged – a ragged form of uneven economic development and labour market segmentation – new mines, mills, factories and railway camps dotted the country. Three million new Canadians came into the country to work in the new industries and produce the "prairie gold" as the Canadian west opened up for agricultural development and settlement. To Canadianize the immigrant became, for some educators, the "one great commanding problem" of the time.[7] People flooded into the cities altering the balance between city and rural dweller. Canadians were now confronted with another "learning challenge" – how to cope with urban life and how to preserve the rural way of life. Industrialization, immigration, urbanization – these were the critical societal learning challenges for Canadians.

Historians have characterized the relationship between capital and labour in this period as especially conflictual and turbulent.[8] Workplace restructuring and transformation confronted Canadian workers with a diverse set of problems. In south central Ontario, for instance, skilled workers resisted the introduction of Taylorist technological changes.[9] More characteristic, however, were the strikes initiated by the "less skilled" workers in the coal fields of Cape Breton, Nova Scotia, and British Columbia, the west coast fishing industry, and the Québec textile industry. Strikes in these industries were often violently repressed. Perhaps one of the most evocative metaphors from this period can be drawn from Cape Breton. Protesting their wretched conditions in the community and work site, over 3,000 striking UMWA miners planned a giant parade in Glace Bay, July 1909. After listening to some speeches at the parade grounds, they marched, led by their leaders. Things went smoothly until they reached Cadegan's Bank, which separates the towns of Glace Bay and Dominion. As they crossed the bridge, the leaders were shocked to find a machine gun mounted on the steps of the Roman Catholic Church of Immaculate Conception, the army poised nearby, ready to fire.[10]

Canadian workers did, indeed, reflect on the critical themes that swashbuckling corporate capitalism was placing on the "curriculum." A multiplicity of labour's schools ("pure and simple" international craft unionism, labourism, Christian socialism, syndicalism, revolutionary Marxism) competed for an audience fragmented by region, nature of industry, ethnicity and gender. But for a brief historic moment in Canadian working class history, the Winnipeg General Strike of 1919, an eclectic radicalism infused with new social principles – the exuberance of wartime radicalism, international working class advance – created a climate in which proletarian victory seemed possible.[11] Education, we have said, must always be considered in attempts to understand the larger process of social conflict and change. We can now provide a synoptic look at workers' education in Winnipeg from 1912 to 1921, with a side-glance to Cape Breton, before turning to an analysis of conflicting discursive fields within "adult education" during this time.

What sites did the resilient Winnipeg workers create for the "organization of enlightenment"? What critical themes did they examine? What were the learning outcomes? The most eclectic of the workers' educational projects in Winnipeg was the People's Forum. Originating with the social gospel/social work activities in the city's legendary north end in 1910, the originators of the Forum included people who, during the war years, would become convinced of the need to create a fundamentally different society – a cooperative commonwealth. Labour's pedagogues included the Christian pacifist J. S. Woodsworth, Frances Beynon, a radical feminist fired from the *Grain Growers' Guide* for anti-war and anti-capitalist activities, and A. V. Thomas, her brother-in-law, also fired from the conservative *Manitoba Free Press*.

Operating independently of the Winnipeg school system until 1914, the People's Forum held regular Sunday meetings in local theatres until it floundered in 1917, largely because of the commitment of many of its leaders to radical political activities. Throughout the turbulent years from 1912 to 1917, *The Voice*, a workers' paper which criticized capitalist abuses from an essentially Christian ethical position, carried weekly reports of events at the People's Forum in Winnipeg, and in a host of others in surrounding communities. The workers' press announced lectures and meetings and often carried verbatim lecture texts. The People's Forum, evidence suggests, encouraged participatory engagement, discussion always following lectures. The workers' press did not provide equal coverage of other educational forums – the YMCA and the University of Manitoba.

Judging from the reports in *The Voice*, the Forum debated a wide range of critical themes. Speakers called for increased political involvement because "our system of government places great power in the hands of a few men," and numerous speakers addressed the issue of militarism, the need for social reconstruction and the need to teach children in their own language. The latter theme signals the presence of an active ethnic presence in Winnipeg's north end. The anti-militarist theme offended some school board members and forced the Forum committee into some compromises. But a number of forums, featuring men like the controversial Methodist and social gospeller Salem Bland of Wesley Theological College (Winnipeg was the leading centre of the social gospel in Canada), continued to indict the war.

By the autumn of 1917, the leadership of the Forum had dispersed, but workers' educational activities continued unabated. Rejecting the People's Forum's affiliation with the public school system and "bourgeois reformism," The Winnipeg Trades and Labour Council (WTLC) announced in September, 1917, a series of Sunday afternoon lectures, featuring the "radical wing" of the People's Forum (J. S. Woodsworth, Fred Dixon, Salem Bland and William Ivens, the Labour Church's instigator). The People's Forum and the Labour Church, bridged by the WTLC lecture series, form a continuum of educational activity. "Together," Maciejko claims, they formed a "consistent and concerted program of workers' education initiated by the radicals and sustained by popular support."[12] By the end of 1918, it seems safe to conclude, Winnipeg workers had been enlightened to the point where they believed that alternatives to capitalism were, indeed, necessary and possible.

As working class militancy quickened in 1918 and 1919, provoking great fear among the middle and upper classes (the notorious "Red Scare"), the educational campaign among workers intensified. Organized in March, 1919, after the epochal Western Labour Conference, the One Big Union (OBU) sought to unify all workers into a single union which could achieve its purposes, economic and political, through general strikes. It would embody proletarian solidarity. The revolutionary syndicalism, though alienating highly skilled craft unions, caught the imagination of many Canadian workers for a flickering historical moment.[13] The linkage between the OBU and the Labour Church was strengthened when more conservative unionists took over the WTLC and the *Western Labour News*. Ivens, who would be jailed in the aftermath of the Winnipeg General Strike, left the *News* and joined the staff of the *OBU Bulletin*, and the latter became the vehicle for informing people of Labour Church activities.

Perhaps the most significant development in Winnipeg in September, 1919, was the Labour Church and OBU's call for the formation of a Labour College for Winnipeg after the bitter defeat of the General Strike of May and June. A parallel initiative, several years later, occurred in Nova Scotia – particularly among the radical coal miners, who were very interested in workers' education. The workers wanted a permanent provincial Labour College that would draw on the expertise of teachers and college professors.[14] Nova Scotia workers would not get what they wanted, and would have to wait until St. Francis Xavier University provided educational services for workers in the late 1920s and 1930s. But St. Francis had its own agenda, and one major item was to quell the insurrection of community knowledge and political action in industrial Cape Breton.[15]

The OBU, itself, was also active in organizing classes and lectures. Of all the classes conducted by the OBU, those in economics were the most popular. From the beginning, the educational classes of the OBU were considered to be preliminary to the establishment of a Labour College in Winnipeg. With this dream in mind, Winnipeg workers wrote to the firebrand Scottish radical John McLean of the Glasgow Labour College, and also to the Rand School of Social Science. The international labour movement – at least its more radical wing – clearly thought they needed a permanent school to nurture their brand of oppositional consciousness. But a Canadian Labour College would not materialize until the 1960s, and then only under the watchful eye of reformist trade union bureaucrats running the Canadian Labour Congress.

Workers' education, however, was not confined to the Forum, the Labour Church and the OBU. Radical political parties – an integral if fractious part of the configuration of labour's schools – were also involved in the movement in Winnipeg. The Socialist Party of Canada (SPC), tracing its origins to Winnipeg in 1890, but having its deepest roots amongst the hard rock miners of BC's mountains, rigorously and dogmatically schooled its resolute vanguard in Marxist axioms. Animated by a chiliastic vision of capitalism's inevitable end, the SPC saw the education of the proletariat as its ultimate political function. Reform for SPCers was "powder sprinkled over the festering sores of that organism called human society."[16] They were convinced that workers needed only to learn Marx's analysis of capitalism and they would become revolutionaries. By 1910, the SPC was conducting study classes in economics (the curriculum focused on the need to abolish the wage system), and in Canadian history and English for immigrants. Like the Forum meetings, SPC classes were noted for audience participation. Undeniably, however, the sectarianism and impossibilism of the SPC (it eschewed, in principle if not always in practice, working with trade unions) was unattractive to many British-born Winnipeg members of the radical movement. Still, there can be no doubt that SPC leaders' analysis of a class-polarized society resonated deeply amongst many workers in the tense years at the end of the World War I.

Other small but not insignificant socialist parties like the Social Democratic Party (SDP) – which split from the SPC in 1911 – also arranged some evening classes during the 1912-1913 session. The SDP's brand of socialism, its tone and tactics, was more palatable to the broad-based Winnipeg left. The SDP juggled its Marxist principles and its commitment to work unceasingly for reforms, an approach that brought it considerable support, including that of eastern European immigrants. But its adult educational work was accomplished primarily through the People's Forum, and some of its members worked with the youth wing. Other parties – the Dominion Labour party and the Independent Labour Party – engaged only sporadically in regular educational programs under their direct auspices. Their members were, however, involved in the educational programs of the People's Forum, OBU, and Labour Church, testifying to the importance placed on adult education by those actively seeking to restructure society in accordance with some variation of socialist principles.

What emerges from this synopsis of the educational activities of radical workers in Winnipeg, says Maciejko, is not a "picture of random or purposeless activity, but a pattern with direction and consistency."[17] According to Allen Mills, J. S. Woodsworth believed that: "The making of socialists . . . was an intellectual activity, requiring for its success a constant appeal to the spoken and written word. Socialism would arrive . . . through voluntary action that derived from the power of clear, methodological, and rational argument itself."[18] Many radical workers shared Woodsworth's faith in the power of intellectual activity as integral to the "organization of action." There was widespread recognition that education was essential to the change process itself. Even H. G. Fester, chair of the Ontario section of the WEA and committed to the WEA's program of "organized classes," recognized that radical organizations deserved a place in the "scheme of workers' education." Though labeling the radicals' educational work as purely propagandist, Fester admitted that their numerous publications and educational activities had awakened some minds out of lethargy.[19] From this knowledge of the power of ideas in the political battle came the proposal to place on the entrance of the OBU's Plebs Hall the inscription: "Read, Study and Investigate, for in the application of the meaning of these words, we will conquer."[20]

But the workers' movement, in Winnipeg and elsewhere in Canada, did not conquer Canadian society. In May and June, 1919, approximately 25,000 men and women struck in sympathy with the embattled workers of the city's building and metal trades; in other cities of Canada, workers staged massive support strikes. These political actions which had social and political learning outcomes, testify to the success of the teachings of labour's schools. Yet, the strike was crushed, leaders associated with the OBU were jailed (the OBU collapsed in 1920), the fragility of utopian hopes was revealed, and the basic reformism of the labour movement was exposed. Labour radicalism called forth its dialectical opposite, reaction from the dominant order: The Citizens' Committee of 1000 moved to suppress the strikers, special police raided labour halls and strike leaders' homes, and "foreign Bolsheviks" were jailed. Viewed through the workers' learning lens, we could hypothesize that the Winnipeg General Strike taught workers how dangerous their knowledge was, the enormous difficulty of achieving a collective identity, and the fierce resistance to transformative action regarding basic power relations in the society. The General Strike of 1919 led, like the collapse of the Knights of Labour in an earlier decade, into a new period of profound disillusion within working class experience.

## Workers' Education and Competing Discursive Fields

Our picture of the adult education discursive field in the first two decades of the twentieth century is not yet complete. Writing two years after the Winnipeg General Strike, Father Jimmy Tompkins captured something of the sentiment present amongst thoughtful university educators when he declared in his pamphlet, *Knowledge for the People*:

> Old ways of thinking have been broken up and a new spirit today can no more be doubted than we were permitted to doubt, during the years between 1914 and 1918, that we were at war. Nowhere is this new spirit more in evidence than in the field of Education. No other idea has so gripped the people of the whole world as the desire for more knowledge, better intellectual training, and better organized effort in their various callings. It has gripped them *en masse* and without regard to condition, class or circumstances. Men and women everywhere are clamouring for the equal opportunity that education and intellectual training give.[21]

Significantly, Tompkins pointed approvingly to developments within the global university extension movement and the WEA; he did not mention any of the forms of adult education present within the workers' movement itself. What Tompkins' ringing proclamation, framed within a liberal progressive discourse, veils is precisely how the universities and other emergent adult education forms (like Frontier College) understood the social crisis and what constituted legitimate educational practice. If labour radicalism – the outcome of informal and nonformal social and

political learning processes – confronted the coercive appa-
ratus of the state, these same workers also faced an ideological opposition which would, directly or indirectly, contest
their educational practice.

The Canadian university extension movement emerged
in the first two decades of the twentieth century. It, too, recognized the potential of adult education in resolving social
conflict. Although Queen's University organized some tutorial classes in 1889, the University of Alberta Extension
Department, created in 1912, was really the first in the field.
The University of Toronto organized its Extension
Department in 1920. It provides a useful focal point, since it
sponsored the first WEA tutorial classes *for* workers and is
considered Canada's most prestigious centre of higher learning.

In a three-page document simply entitled "University
Extension," written in 1922, the University of Toronto presented its understanding of the nature and purpose of adult
education. This seemingly innocuous document provides crucial insights into the way the university, as the socially and
historically designated space for legitimate knowledge production and dissemination, was constructing adult education.
From the opening line, the text is pervaded by a profound
sense of danger and crisis. "At this moment," the anonymous
author(s) declared, there is a "crisis in the whole world of
education." How was this crisis perceived? Public schools and
the technical training provided by universities had left out
the "most important part" of education. Neither had developed the "power of thinking" or "useful criticism," but more
significantly, neither had built up a "thoughtful, comprehend-
ing human spirit."[22] The latter task was most urgent.

The crisis in education, for the text's author(s), only
reflected a much deeper crisis – that of a class-polarized society. The author(s) contended that what now existed in
Canada were two more or less unrelated standards of think-

ing and speaking. Canada was a severed society, speaking two warring ideological languages. "There is an immense danger to a country in the existence of two languages, the language of the cultivated and the language of the street, neither of which is really comprehensible to the other."[23] The choice of the street/cultivated metaphor is significant. The languages of social transformation – products of workers' own learning and experience – are consigned to the street, the realm of the undisciplined, the untrained, the untutored, and the rebellious. Indeed, one catches in the text's identification of adult education with "formalized" instruction by "trained" tutors (adult education began with the offering of university courses) the notion that only knowledge cultivated by the professor/gardener is legitimate. For the author(s) contend that "if it could be brought about that more or less the same proportion of every class could be found in the ranks of thoughtful cultivated people, an immense stride would have been made in the abolition of class differences."[24]

It is imperative that the university extend its "higher culture" to those classes previously neglected. Because the "whole basis of national unity rests upon the theory of the nation being an aggregation of persons who, on the whole, think alike, and it is very difficult for two sets of people to think alike who speak more or less different languages and think in different categories," a "large expansion" of adult education is called for. Incorporating the workers into this higher culture is intimately bound up with the extension metaphor: to extend means to control. The fundamental motivation for extending adult education is not, as suggested by Tompkins and "University Extension," to provide what workers want (they demand, we just respond), but to promote social harmony between capital and labour. This is to be accomplished through the idealist project of creating a standardized, uniform, monologic culture. But this monologic voice can only speak its values by repressing workers' polyphonous voices. Adult education, as constructed by university extension, had given itself an impossible task (like that of public schooling in mid-nineteenth-century Canada) of equalizing the classes without abolishing class domination.

Why was the WEA successfully established in Toronto at the end of the World War I? To be sure, some working men had asked the University of Toronto to cooperate in establishing an organization similar to the British WEA. But working class people were not the main impetus behind the founding of the WEA in Toronto. All of the key players – W. L. Grant, principal of Upper Canada College; Professors R. M. McIver and W. S. Milner; and Arthur Glazebrook, an exchange broker – believed that the foundations of democracy were under siege in a crassly materialistic age. Clearly alarmed by the Russian Revolution, the Winnipeg General Strike, and the OBU, and startled by the enormously increased strike activity, rapid growth of trade unionism, and expansion of labour political action in Ontario, these middle-class academics "sought to use the Association as a means to curb the spread of radicalism."[25]

In an essay, "The Education of the Working Man," published in the prestigious *Queen's Quarterly* in 1919, W. L. Grant spoke gravely of the "flood of ideas" sweeping over the "civilized world."[26] Nineteenth-century *laissez-faire* individualism had collapsed and only the "cash nexus" seemed to be holding society together. How could democracy endure? The working class wanted, in his view, a "new *concordat* between Capital and Labour and the State." They wanted to be owners alike in industry and politics. But only those who were "educated" were fit to take part in guiding the destinies of the state. Uneducated working people and citizens, Grant believed, leapt uncritically at every new idea. "Ideas without education" were "very dangerous fodder. Ideas without education mean the triumph of the half-baked; and the results of the triumph of the half-baked are manifest to the world in

Russia today." Education, as construed by Grant, had to sub-
jugate alternative knowledge forms produced in learning
sites outside the control of those with disciplined and cultivated minds. If the "broad sunlight of education" were to be
spread over the workers' miasma "of incoherent ideas," then
adult education had to be organized. And the university
would be the centre, "the splendid fertilizing nucleus."
Grant's constitution of adult education is neither innocent
nor value-free. The call for "organized" (formal) adult education under the disciplinary eye of the trained tutor must,
necessarily, exclude and delegitimate "unorganized" (nonfor-
mal/informal) learning. This tactic on the conceptual level is
integral to the political struggle to ensure that the "pervert-
ed vision" of Bolshevism (now a symbol for dangerous learning) does not "widen itself to take in the whole country."
Grant celebrated the British WEA – its historic links with
Oxford – precisely because of its moderation. "The WEA,"
Grant opined, "is thus the educational side of the Labour
Movement; a great school of Political Science for the working classes." But the WEA, in Canada as in Britain, was only
one of labour's schools, a good antidote to class struggle.[27]

All the educators who supported the WEA insisted that
the teaching be done by university professors. "It is the university, after all," declared Glazebrook, "that contains the
treasury of knowledge and the training in method that are
required."[28] This would be a matter of some controversy.
Writing to Grant on 13 October, 1921, classics professor W.
S. Milner thought that the "success of the WEA as an educational ideal was seriously imperilled."[29] The controversy,
one of many to dog the WEA's path until its demise in the
late 1940s, was over union activist James Ballantyne's desire
to teach a course in Marxian economics. Though not deny-
ing the right of the university to deal with Marx, Milner
thought it both unwise and absurd to exercise this right.
How could the university support a teacher from the work-

ers' own ranks? Despairing and disconsolate, Milner took his stand for the "culture of mind and spirit." The "unhappy truth," as he saw it, was that the WEA had fallen into the hands of "Labour that is more anxious for power than for culture, and that the spiritual force of the movement is on the ebb."[30]

The WEA was, in fact, contested terrain throughout its history. Conflicting visions of adult education – its purpose and process – would be articulated by multiple voices. In the early years of the Association, a number of working men (like the Irishman Alf MacGowan of the International Typographical Union) believed that workers with more knowledge could help improve the existing political and social system. They hoped it would be improved through a workers' educational movement that increased workers' understanding of political and social issues. These worker activists shared the academics' faith that truth could be examined in an unbiased way – the grand vision of the British WEA tutorial movement.[31]

All agreed, too, that a technical education was not enough, and that workers needed access to broader knowledge. Significantly, however, other workers emphasized the need for social justice and attacked the limitations of education in a class society and insisted on the social and collective purpose of the WEA. The redoubtable Winnipeg labour movement shared this latter conviction. In 1915 they had met with University of Manitoba Professor J. A. Dale to discuss the formation of a chapter of the WEA. From the start they were suspicious. The University of Manitoba, the committee claimed, was for the rich and provided only "scraps of knowledge" for workers. After the meeting the Winnipeg Trades and Labour Congress (TLC) decided not to support the WEA because they had to deal with professors who were in the grip of capitalist ideology. The WEA was unable to establish itself in Winnipeg until 1938. This mutual suspicion between the labour movement and the universities is one of the important sub-texts in the history of Canadian, as well as global, workers' education.

In discussing this disparity of views, Redforth and Sangster observe:

> Common language such as "education for citizenship" masked some very significant differences between the aims of the educationalists and those of the labour activists. The class differences of the two groups do much to explain the divergent meanings behind their words. On the one hand, the educationalists saw the WEA as, in part, an experiment in social control. They sought to use their positions as academics and intellectuals to maintain existing power relations in society. On the other hand, the labour activists hoped to further the cause of labour and to help redress the imbalance of power in society. These fundamental differences existed within the Association from the start. Inevitably, as time progressed, the underlying tensions would surface.[32]

In March, 1922, the *Canadian Forum* noted that throughout Canada workers were "suspicious" of both the WEA and Frontier College. What was at the root of worker suspicion of Frontier College? Alfred Fitzpatrick, a disillusioned Presbyterian minister, organized the Reading Camp Association in 1899 (it would become Frontier College in 1919). For Fitzpatrick, the *laissez-faire* state of the late nineteenth and early twentieth centuries had neglected the men working in isolated and wretched railway, lumbering and mining camps (the "bunkhouse men"). Through silence and lack of intervention, the Canadian state had legitimated the exploitation of the campmen's labour and their maintenance as uneducated wage-slaves. Nor did the trade unions pay any attention to these men. Continually calling on the state to intervene in deploying resources for neglected adult learners (his dominant metaphor), Fitzpatrick would be repeatedly rebuffed, despite his powerful moral argument that the state derived its funds from frontier industries.

In his text, *The University in Overalls*, Fitzpatrick described the origins of Frontier College as an educational mission to the bunkhouse men. Fitzpatrick's adult educational discourse is a unique mix of radical and conservative elements. He was appalled at the elitism of Canadian universities and criticized them for their ivory-tower separation from the real world of the hand. "Classes," he declared, "must be held, not only in the schools and universities, but in the shops, on the works, in the camps and fields and settlements of the frontier."[33] The University of Toronto could hardly find the resources to run a few tutorial classes! In an eloquent chapter, "Education and the Frontier Camps," Fitzpatrick argued that the urban-based middle class had appropriated the labour of those toiling and sweating in the mines and camps. Their wealth production, he said, had endowed the resources used by the middle and upper class in the cities. Fitzpatrick castigated the philanthropists who endowed the colleges and ignored the "living and housing conditions of their own workers in the camps and mills." The task of educationists was nothing less than "to devise ways and means of taking the school and college to the frontier."[34] The men of the camps needed justice, not charity.

Fitzpatrick's educational vision is rooted in the socially regenerative assumptions of late Victorian society.[35] He argued that education was for all men, and not for a privileged class alone. Appropriating Marx's notion of humanization through labour, but not his radical politics, Fitzpatrick – the early twentieth century social gospeller – thought the solution to structurally rooted problems lay with the redemption of the individual through empathetic provision of basic adult education (literacy and citizenship training). This is a paternalistic and moralistic vision. Yet, Fitzpatrick stood outside the establishment, unlike the patrons of the Mechanics' Institutes and supporters of the Toronto WEA, with the voiceless and the mute. His discourse was patronizing but spoken with a deeply humanistic accent. His social gospel ideology moved him toward the neglected while simultaneously constraining his educational practice, repressing more overtly political education for social transformation and a nonconformist conception of citizenship.

But there can be no doubt that, like W. L. Grant and other early university supporters of the WEA, Fitzpatrick feared the "Bolsheviks." When strikes swept the camps in 1919, he contended that the labourer-teachers' activities would determine whether the camps would produce "Lenins or Lincolns."[36]

Working under the banner, "Welfare-Instruction-Canadianizing-Leadership," the labourer-teachers' objectives were (a) to educate the worker and give him a fighting chance, (b) to educate and citizenize [sic] the immigrant, and (c) to meet the "Red agitator" on his own ground. Fitzpatrick emerged from the social dislocation and political ferment of the war more convinced than ever that the labourer-teacher could exercise a moral-redemptive influence on the "dangerous foreigners."

Fitzpatrick seemed to believe that, with a little education, a camp worker would cease his "evil" habits. He envisioned his Reading Camp instructors as models of "staunch Canadians," inculcating Anglo-Saxon and Protestant values. Thus, with some education and paternalistic guidance from the "right" sector of society (he recruited middle-class university students), not only would the campmen's lives be improved but this achievement would help stabilize the social order. Fitzpatrick, in spite of his humanism, instrumentalized adult education in the interests of social harmony.

Linking Fitzpatrick's commitment to "Canadianize," the "Red Scare," and the labour movement, Donald Avery speculates that organizations like Frontier College aggravated the immigrants' sense of their own cultural identification. Shunned and patronized by traditional nativist institutions, alienated immigrant workers turned to groups that sought to transform Canadian society through revolution – the IWW, OBU, and Canadian Communist Party.[37]

## Concluding Critical Theorems

The struggles of workers in the turbulent decades of discord can be viewed as a contest between supporters of conflicting visions of what constitutes valid enlightenment, empowerment, and transformative action. A multiplicity of labour's schools offered their vision of the purpose of adult education in a society viewed as essentially conflictual. Outside labour's schools, adult educators offered their vision of adult education in a society viewed as essentially harmonious (though momentarily divided).

Adult education does not have an essence; competing discourses struggle with one another for hegemony. Adult education is always both normative and descriptive, and does not mean the same thing to everyone.

Particular discursive practices are intimately bound up with social power and control. Adult education discourse sets the limits of what counts as authentic educational practice. This theorem seems borne out in our analysis of how the legitimate and authoritative formal educational institutions (university extension and WEA) attempted to constitute their particular discourse as normative. The success of this manoeuvre to establish discursive hegemony is bound up with the power relations of the society – the ability of the dominant order to block or manage, coercively and conceptually, the autonomous contestatory learning processes erupting in a multiplicity of learning sites (work place, community, trade union, political party, newspaper, and so on).

While a simplistic social control model of the WEA or university extension is inadequate to grasp the complexities of workers' education, the extension metaphor signals a move on the part of the dominant order to manage and constrain knowledge and action that threatens social order.

## Notes

1. Michael R. Welton, "The Depths of Despondency: The Struggle for Autonomous Workers' Education in the Vancouver WEA, 1942-1948," *CASAE History Bulletin* (May, 1986); Michael R. Welton, ed., *Knowledge for the People: the Struggle for Adult Learning in English-Speaking Canada, 1928-1973* (Toronto: OISE Press, 1986).

2. Gregory Keeley and Brian Palmer, *Dreaming of What Might Be: the Knights of Labour in Ontario, 1880-1980* (Cambridge: Cambridge University Press, 1982); Brian Palmer, *Working-Class Experience, the Rise and Reconstitution of Canadian Labour, 1800-1980* (Toronto: Butterworth, 1983).

3. B. Fay, *Critical Social Science: Liberation and its Limits* (Ithaca: Cornell University Press, 1987); W. J. Maciejko, "Read, Study and Investigate: Workers Education in Winnipeg, 1912-1921," *CASAE History Bulletin* (May, 1986); B. Simon, "Can Education Change Society?", in J. D. Wilson, ed., *An Imperfect Past: Education and Society in Canadian History* (Vancouver: University of British Columbia Centre for the Study of Curriculum and Instruction, 1984).

4. D. Stewart, *Adult Learning in America: Edward Lindeman and His Agenda for Life-Long Learning* (Malabar FL: Robert Kreiger, 1987).

5. K. Rockhill, "Ideological Solidification of Liberalism in University Adult Education: Confrontation over Workers' Education in the U.S.A.," in R. Taylor, K. Rockhill and R. Fieldhouse, *University Adult Education in England and the U.S.A.* (Croom Helm, 1985), pp. 175-220.

6. Michel Foucault, *Power/Knowledge: Selected Interviews and Other Writings, 1972-1977* (New York: Pantheon/Random House, 1980).

7. J. T. Anderson, *The Education of the New Canadian* (Toronto: James Dent and Sons, 1918); A. Fitzpatrick, *The University in Overalls* (Toronto: Frontier College Press, 1920); J. S. Woodsworth, *Strangers within our Gates* (Toronto: University of Toronto Press, 1909), reprinted 1972.

8. R. Brown and Ramsay Cook, *Canada: A Nation Transformed* (Toronto: McClelland and Stewart, 1974; S. Jamieson, *Times of Trouble: Labour Unrest and Industrial Conflict in Canada, 1900-1966* (Ottawa: Information Canada, 1986).

9. Craig Heron and R. Storey, eds., *On the Job, Confronting the Labour Process* (Kingston and Montreal: McGill-Queen's University Press, 1986).

10. J. Mellor, *The Company Store: James Bryson McLachlan and the Cape Breton Coal Miners, 1899-1919* (Toronto: Doubleday, 1983).

11. Palmer, *op. cit.*

12. Maciejko, *op. cit.*, p. 9.

13. A. R. McCormack, *Reformers, Rebels and Revolutionaries: The Western Canada Radical Movement, 1899-1919* (Toronto: University of Toronto Press, 1977).

14. G. MacDonald, "'Workers' Education in Nova Scotia: Illuminating/ Learning/History," *CASAE History Bulletin* (May, 1986).

15. Moses Coady, *Masters of Their Own Destiny* (New York: Harper and Row, 1939).

16. Quoted in McCormack, *op. cit.*, p. 54.

17. Maciejko, *op. cit.*, p. 13.

18. A. Mills, "Cooperation and Community in the Thought of J. S. Woodsworth," *Labour/Le Travail* 14 (1984), pp. 103-120, p. 105.

19. H. G. Fester, "Workers' Education in Canada," *Proceedings of the [US] National Conference of Social Work* (1924).

20. Central Labour Council of the One Big Union [OBU], "Executive Minutes," 6 January, 1920.

21. J. Tompkins, *Knowledge for the People* (Antigonish: private publication, 1921), p. 3

22. "University Extension," University of Toronto Extension Papers, 1922, File 1, Box Print Materials, University of Toronto Archives, no pagination.

23. *Ibid.*

24. *Ibid.*

25. I. Radforth and J. Sangster, "The Struggle for Autonomous Workers' Education: The Workers' Educational Association in Ontario, 1917-1951," in M. R. Welton, ed., *Knowledge for the People*, pp. 73-96, p. 75.

26. W. L. Grant, "The Education of the Working Man," *Queen's Quarterly* (October, 1919), p. 160.

27. R. Fieldhouse, "The 1908 Report: Antidote to Class Struggle?" in S. Harrop, ed., *Oxford and Working-Class Education* (University of Nottingham, Department of Adult Education, 1987), pp. 30–47.

28. R. Glazebrook, "Memorandum to Educational Commission, 1921," *W. L. Grant Papers*, Box 2, Public Archives of Canada.

29. W. S. Milner, "Letter to W. L. Grant, 13 October, 1921," *W. L. Grant Papers*, Box 2, Public Archives of Canada.

30. *Ibid.*

31. R. Fieldhouse, "The Problems of Objectivity, Social Purpose and Ideological Commitment in English University Adult Education," in Taylor et al., *op. cit.*, pp. 29–51.

32. Radforth and Sangster, *op. cit.*, p. 78.

33. Fitzpatrick, *op. cit.*, p. ix.

34. *Ibid.*, p. 42.

35. Ramsay Cook, *The Regenerators: Social Criticism in Late Victorian English Canada* (Toronto: University of Toronto Press, 1985).

36. G. Cook, "Educational Justice for the Campmen: Alfred Fitzpatrick and the Foundation of Frontier College," in Welton, *Knowledge for the People*, pp. 35–51, p. 47.

37. Donald Avery, *Dangerous Foreigners: European Immigrant Workers and Labour Radicalism in Canada, 1896-1932* (Toronto: McClelland and Stewart, 1979).

# About Face

The Social Construction of Homelessness
Among Women in "Toronto the Good"

## Diane E. Meaghan

This ethnographic study examines the relevance of social
determinants to understand homelessness among women.
The impact of globalization that has restructured economies,
reinvented institutions, and undermined social services is
investigated to assess the effect of a transformed Canadian
economy on gendered patterns of homelessness. Marginalized by government policy, underrepresented in academic
debates and overlooked in mainstream society, it was anticipated that the pathways to homelessness could be traced to
macro-structural factors through the examination of the life
narratives of homeless women. Thirty-seven homeless
women in the greater Toronto area were surveyed concerning their history of homelessness, the factors that led to their
homelessness, their perceptions of current needs and
resources and their plans for the future. To provide a comprehensive picture, interviews were also conducted with
social workers, community activists, health care professionals,
politicians and spokespersons for non-governmental organizations together with the use of secondary sources of information.

Similar to emerging theories of political economy, this
study views homelessness as shaped by macro-level political
and economic trends interacting at a micro-level with specific personal concerns.[1] Recent research has concentrated on

the individual deficit thesis, attempting to explain how personal problems such as chemical dependence and mental illness lead to stress, marginalization and an inability to obtain or sustain housing.[2] Social work literature is especially devoid of structural explanations, often resorting to individual, pathology-based interpretations of homelessness.[3] Such explanations fail to consider the political and economic context in which homelessness has exploded over the past decade. Individual factors are not irrelevant. Losing one's job severs social relations and reduces motivation to engage in socially accepted behaviour.[4] Lack of housing affects both physical and psychological health.[5] The etiological components of homelessness begin a downward spiral from which it is difficult to escape, as unconventional behaviour results in greater isolation and the likelihood of entrenched homelessness.[6] Nonetheless, the contemporary pattern of homelessness is systemic, oppressive[7] and largely the result of problems of poverty and increasing long-term joblessness.[8] This approach views homelessness as socially constructed and originating in the structures of society.[9] Increasingly, attention is being paid to social explanations in which homelessness is seen as a cause rather than the result of social stress and disorder.[10]

Although it is acknowledged that homelessness is experienced differently according to gender, few studies have focused on women; almost none have used gender as an organizing category of analysis.[11] Research typically operates within a gender-neutral framework or subsumes women within families and thus fails to deal with their unique experiences. Within an increasingly integrated and rationalized global economy, corporations have sought cheap labour outside Canada to displace semi-skilled and unskilled domestic workers. Organizations have become more interested in a neoliberal agenda of welfare and social service "reforms" (that have a disproportionate impact on the lives of women and children through a decrease in social benefits), and less concerned to conserve income redistribution policies that assist workers to purchase local goods and services and less interested in maintaining the health and welfare of the domestic workforce.[12]

Today, homelessness has a face. It is increasingly poor, vulnerable and female. Homelessness is visited primarily upon those who have had negatively identifiable childhood experiences. Focusing on social difficulties, Johnson determined that such issues were antecedent conditions of homelessness among women.[13] Koegel et. al., found that most homeless adults encountered significant personal problems as children. Nearly half of the homeless in their study lived apart from parents during their childhood, and one quarter had been placed in foster care or institutional care or both. Approximately 60 percent of the homeless indicated that the family with which they had grown up received welfare or that they lacked the basic necessities.[14] The link between personal oppression, particularly a history of victimization in abusive relationships and homelessness has also been established.[15] In addition to childhood difficulties, homelessness is experienced more frequently by young and elderly women. Keigher and Pratt's work underscore the fact that women have become increasingly vulnerable due to marked reductions in public housing construction, a deterioration of existing public housing and a substantial decline in the number of low cost housing facilities.[16]

## Poverty as an Underlying Cause of Homelessness

A recent U.S. study found that by age thirty-five nearly one-third of the population had lived a year or more in poverty; by age sixty-five over half of Americans spent at least a year in poverty; by age eighty-five, two-thirds of the population had encountered poverty.[17] Far from being the fate of only a marginalized "underclass," poverty was found to be a phe-

nomenon that crossed race, ethnicity, religion, age and geographic boundaries. Many Canadians pride themselves on
being different from our neighbours to the south, especially
with regard to matters of compassion and equity for the disadvantaged; however, studies indicate that this is not the case.
Reports by entities as diverse as the Toronto Drop-in
Coalition,[18] The National Council on Welfare,[19] and the
government of the City of Toronto[20] acknowledge that social
benefits have not kept pace with the cost-of-living, causing
more people to fall below the poverty line.

In Canada, the shrinking of the "social wage" began in
earnest in 1985 when Brian Mulroney de-indexed Family
Allowances. In 1990, the assault continued with the federal
Expenditure Control Plan that limited transfer payments to
the provinces for health and social assistance. The first
Chrétien budget continued cuts to Unemployment Insurance; the second budget under Finance Minister Paul
Martin created what he proudly (and correctly) called a program of cuts to social programs "unprecedented in modern
Canadian history."[21] The federal government budgeted a
reduction of transfer payments to the provinces of $16 bil-
lion for health, post secondary education, social assistance
and community services for the period 1996-2000.[22] The
National Council of Welfare suggests that the depth of
poverty in Canada has increased essentially because social
benefits have not kept pace with the cost of living that has
caused recipients to fall below the poverty line.[23] The combination of federal cut-backs in transfer payments to the
provinces, provincial down-loading of services to the municipalities, and the municipalities' inability to address homelessness (combined with landlords' and developers' lobbying
efforts to keep rents high and low-rental housing limited)
created a context in which homelessness for more and more
vulnerable people became inevitable.

Reminiscent of the debates about the English *Poor Laws*

almost two centuries ago, emerging discourses concerning
the poor advocate providing as little as possible under circumstances that are as unpleasant as possible in order to
increase the motive to work.[24] Where that does not work,
criminalization (as with "squeegie kids" and "aggressive"
panhandlers) is an effective fallback position.[25] Consciously
generated myths demonize where the legislatures do not
criminalize the poor. The homeless are stereotyped as lazy at
best, addicted or criminal at worst, and in either case fully
responsible for their own condition.[26] In re-framing poverty
as an individual rather than a societal problem susceptible to
state solutions, business organizations such as the Business
Council on National Issues, right-wing "think tanks" such as
the C. D. Howe and Fraser Institutes, politicians and media
pundits produce a climate of "victim blaming."[27] One mid-
dle-aged, homeless woman states:

> In a way, we are a necessary part of society. When you feel
> badly, you can compare yourself to us. If you look at a wino
> with dirty hair and ragged clothes, you feel better about your-
> self. Maybe you cheated on your taxes, or over-charged some-
> one on a purchase, or didn't tell a cashier that gave you too
> much change. At least you're not as bad as these homeless peo-
> ple, these petty thieves in and out of jail most of their lives.

Economic restrictions and social dislocation have produced
the context for accelerated homelessness. Dealing with the
recession of the early 1990s by reducing government deficits,
deregulating the private sector and downsizing the public sector may improve federal, provincial and municipal credit rat-
ings and thus paint a rosy picture of business growth; however, it reveals little about the human cost of the crisis in social
service, the erosion of economic standards and the quality of
life for many Canadians. The result is that lower-income families (almost half of whom have children and dependent
youths) spend more each month than they earn and the num-

ber of individuals using food banks has doubled during the past eight years.[28] The economically disenfranchised have become more numerous and visible in all Canadian provinces, including Ontario and particularly in "Toronto the Good."[29] Findings from the Mayor's Action Task Force on Homelessness (commonly called "The Golden Report" for its leader Ann Golden) indicated that during the last decade, 47 percent of Toronto's homeless came from outside the city and 14 percent from outside the country.[30] The core of Toronto has become a magnet where both the homeless have migrated and a variety of services are offered. The pull of the magnet is, however, based on false beliefs. In fact, Toronto is falling behind many parts of Ontario including North Bay, Quinte, Halton and Guelph as a suitable place to live.

The poor do not, however, just come from geographically distant places. They also come from the ranks of the previously advantaged. In what they refer to as the "hollowing out of the middle class," researchers with the Canadian Centre for Policy Alternatives have noted that, between 1970 and 1995, the decline suffered by families in the lowest 7 deciles of income amounted to a transfer of $8 billion to the top three deciles.[31] In 1989, for example, the top decile in income made 39 times as much as the lowest decile; by 1995, this inequality had almost tripled with the highest 10 percent of Canadians getting 110 times as much as the lowest 10 per cent.[32] The impact on families is even more devastating. The National Council on Welfare reports that, in 1973, the richest 10 per cent of Canadian families with children under eighteen made 21 times the amount of the lowest 10 per cent; by 1996, this ratio had ballooned to 314 times the income of the poorest 10 per cent. The effects of the assault on the middle class have also been documented by the Centre for Social Justice. Whereas in 1973, 60 per cent of the Canadian population was identified as middle class, the proportion had shrunk to 44 per cent by 1996. While it is true that most of Canada's middle class did not become homeless, neither did they climb the social ladder to join the rich. As middle class Canadians slipped down, those beneath them sunk much further.

## The Response from Government

The Keynesian welfare state, won incrementally over the past half-century, is being dismantled and concepts of community solidarity and public morality are being abandoned in the process. Shifts in spending from the public to the private sector, a realignment of tax policy favouring the wealthy and the corporations, and a reduction of the social sector at the expense of the disadvantaged, cohere in a neoliberal vision of society dominated by market forces and uninterested in social responsibility and equity. Governmental responses to homelessness have mainly concentrated on crisis intervention and the use of emergency services. This approach is both expensive and ineffective in reducing and preventing homelessness. Though necessary, shelters pose no solution to the underlying problem of poverty that has recently been intensified by government cuts to welfare, health care, public housing and social services.

The effect of revoking the Canada Assistance Plan (CAP) resulted in a contraction of social assistance, the elimination of funding for new subsidized housing and a decrease in unemployment benefits. It provided inadequate economic levels of maintenance for low-income households with the numbers of those seeking social assistance in Ontario subsequently increasing by 174 percent from 89,050 in 1990, to 220,879 in 1994.[33] The erosion of the income base among low income workers added to a substantial increase in the cost of housing (often well beyond inflation) and can be directly linked to an increase in homelessness. Canadians paid a high price for what the federal government deemed necessary to keep Canada competitive through the Continental (NAFTA) and hemispheric (FTAA) free trade agreement. In 1993, one in five workers had at least one period of unemployment and one in ten held a temporary job. Once used to buffer the impact of economic changes, unemployment insurance was restructured despite the fact that many full-time, career jobs had disappeared. According to Kevin Hayes, economist with the Canadian Labour Congress (CLC), 45 percent of the deficit reduction undertaken was supported from the pockets of those who were unemployed. Their contributions were in the form of lower benefits, shorter coverage periods and a reduction in eligibility from 74 percent in 1990, to less than 36 percent in 2000.[34] Josephine Grey, spokesperson for the Low Income Families Together contends that the Employment Insurance plan also discriminated against single parents, women, visible minorities and the disabled by directing funds for training to individuals who were most likely to obtain a job after upgrading.[35]

The provincial response to this situation (when it does not involve simple denial) is often to attack the poor. Former Ontario Social Services Minister Janet Ecker, has stated that her government's decision to cut welfare payments would assist the homeless by providing an incentive to get off the streets and change their lives.[36] In an effort to brand people as "welfare cheats," the recent introduction of the Ontario government's *Bill 142* anticipated a much greater capacity to reassess eligibility. According to the late Al Palladini, ex-Minister of Tourism, the problem of homelessness is that people huddle on sewer grates and panhandle on the streets, thus tarnishing Toronto's image. His solution was to remove them from the streets.[37] What is clear is that cuts to provincial welfare payments of 21.6 per cent and the tightening of eligibility rules increased poverty, especially among women and children.

In 1998, Ernie Eves, Ontario's Finance Minister before bolting to the international banking industry, issued an ultimatum to municipalities to reduce business property taxes or the province would enact legislation to compel such reductions.[38] The amalgamation of the Borough of East York and the cities of Etobicoke, North York, Scarborough and Toronto (despite the objection of 76 percent of the residents of Metropolitan Toronto in a referendum), downloaded provincial responsibilities onto municipalities by means of an "actual value" method of property tax assessment and a shift from commercial and industrial to residential property tax. Public policy was transformed by the creation of a budgetary shortfall of $2 billion province-wide ($1 billion in Metro Toronto) every three years.[39] Meanwhile, new pressures on municipal budgets have resulted in local services of social housing, parks and recreation, libraries, public transit, roads, garbage collection, welfare systems, law enforcement and a host of others competing with each other in what Thomas Hobbes once called a "war of all against all" to minimize further reductions. "The notion of the collective good is being replaced by individualism, competition and the privatization of state services," according to Dan Anstett, a social worker providing services to homeless families in the east end of Toronto.[40] To this end, the province put social housing at risk with legislation that requires municipalities to pay 100 per cent of the cost.[41] As well, the cancellation of affordable housing construction and the repeal of rent controls on vacant apartments have severely limited current housing options. The implausibly named *Tenant Protection Act* (1999) currently allows landlords to take income criteria into consideration when deciding upon rental applications. This and other changes in landlord-tenant legislation have increased discrimination against single mothers and their children, allowed for rapid eviction and forcing people out of their apartments if they lose their ability to pay their rent even for a short period of time.

The municipality of Metropolitan Toronto made its own contribution to homelessness among low income families by no longer providing special assistance for the last month's rent deposit that resulted in 75 to 90 percent of available affordable apartments in Toronto being excluded for low income individuals.[42] Given that landlords are required to complete a Rental Promissory Note and provide a copy of the deed to demonstrate they own the premises, such bureaucratic complications make renting to people on social assistance undesirable.

## The Impact of Changes in Canadian Political Economy on Homelessness

Canada is the only country in the Western world that does not have a national housing policy; it is also one of the few developed nations that has abdicated its responsibility for social housing. Federal government expenditures on housing totaled $4.1 billion in 1993, with most of these funds directed toward social housing. The federal government ceased to finance new housing in 1993, then capped funding in 1995 for existing housing projects. The Ontario government withdrew the province's contribution to subsidize new housing in 1996, leaving metropolitan Toronto with 36 percent of the province's social housing units and inadequate funds to maintain, much less to advance, the program.[43] Ontario's former Housing Minister, Al Leach, commissioned the last public housing project in 1995. Not only have there been no new initiatives, but on Mr. Leach's watch 15,000 units that would have housed 45,000 people were cancelled.[44] In effect, the federal government downloaded responsibility for social housing onto the provinces, many of which further downloaded the programs onto cash-strapped municipalities across Canada.[45]

Of all the services offloaded onto the municipalities,

social housing has had the greatest impact with the full costs transferred to the level of government least able to afford it.

The number of homeless increased and became more visible when the federal government ceasing to fund public and co-operative housing by turning some 40,000 units over to Ontario provincial management.[46] Taking the federal government's lead to abandon social housing, the Ontario government downloaded the entire inventory of 275,000 units of social housing onto the municipalities.[47] As a result, waiting lists for Toronto public housing increased by more than one-and-a-half times since 1990 and currently comprise half the Ontario waiting list.[48] By year 2001, fewer than 4,000 out of the 80,000 rental units needed will have been constructed.[49] Considering that the construction of rental housing has decreased from 27 to 6 percent between 1989 and 1998, the provincial government's claim that deregulation of rent controls would result in the construction of affordable housing by the private sector has not proven to be the case.[50] The law of supply and demand has created an affordability problem rather than a construction boom of low rental housing. The Center for Equality Rights in Accommodation (CERA) suggests that the most disadvantaged also suffer discrimination in accessing the existing stock of private housing. The most vulnerable individuals are not able to rent affordable units on the market, since half these rental units do not provide accommodation for people on social assistance.[51]

Household expenditures a decade ago were at little over half of total disposable income – today that level has increased to 88 percent due mostly to the cost of housing. Property taxes are a more retrogressive manner of taxation than income taxes since they are not based on ability to pay. Under such tax schemes, lower income households contribute more of their budgets than households with larger incomes, shifting the cost of social benefits from the affluent to less affluent taxpayers. Currently, one in ten households can not obtain housing which meets federal standards without spending a substantial amount of their income. Deregulation has reduced the number of affordable rental units causing some 60 percent of low-income families to spend more than one-third of their total income on housing. The problem is particularly acute among Aboriginals in which three in ten households evidence housing needs.[52] A number of landlords refuse to rent to individuals who spend more than 30 percent of their income on accommodation, increasingly causing people to live in overcrowded conditions and to be subject to eviction.

## The Growing Problem of Women's Poverty and Homelessness

It is estimated that there are about 200,000 homeless people on any given day in Canada. In Toronto, 26,000 use some of the 110 emergency shelters and feeding centres daily. Approximately 4,700 are homeless and 500 of these sleep on the streets.[53] According to the Mayor's Homelessness Action Task Force, an additional 80,000 people are at risk of becoming homeless.[54] It is difficult to say exactly how many of the homeless are women, but comparative data from the United States estimate the proportion to be 52 per cent.[55] During the past twenty years, the number of single-parent and especially mother-led families has increased, with the largest percentage of these families living below the poverty line in Canada, the U.S.A. and Australia. Indeed, single women with children are the fastest growing sub-population of the homeless.[56]

The most recent five-year report by the United Nations suggests that poverty rates among single mothers have risen at a time when welfare payments have been cut, workfare has been introduced and unemployment insurance programs covered fewer individuals.[57] Despite the fact that the rate of unemployment is higher for women, the claims awarded women have decreased by 20 per cent (compared to 16 per cent for men) after the program was revamped by former Human Resources Minister Pierre Pettigrew.[58] Fewer currently qualify for assistance, while those who obtain benefits access them for shorter periods. Critics such as Alexa McDonough, ex-leader of the New Democratic Party, contend that the government has thereby met key performance indicator quotas of 6 per cent or approximately $612 million in social service reductions.[59] Of the approximately four Canadians in ten who currently receive social assistance benefits, reforms have affected more severely women and young people, both of whom are more likely to work part-time and are therefore less likely to qualify for benefits.[60]

In assessing the disparate impact of social spending in Canada, a report released by the National Association of Women and the Law (NAWL) focused on the importance of a gender analysis concerning women's poverty. "More women are poor today than in 1993, and their poverty is deeper," claims Margot Young, Associate Professor of Law at Laval University and a NAWL Steering Committee member.[61] Cutbacks to government programs fall disproportionately on women, "increasing their load of unpaid care-giving work."[62] Single mothers with children under the age of seven, a group disproportionately affected by government cut-backs to social assistance and other social programs have a poverty rate of 82 per cent, with incomes almost $9,000 under the poverty line.

Homeless women lack more than shelter and food. They are without a range of social and economic resources. The Ontario government's recent initiatives to revoke pay equity have deprived 100,000 of the lowest-paid women of the money owing them. Since Ontario's Conservative government was elected, provincial welfare rolls have dropped each month with almost 400,000 fewer people currently collecting welfare in Toronto.[63] Through the province's reduction of the family support plan, shelter funds, hospital and educational services, "the Tories have added to the desperation of half a million children who have fallen into ever-worsening hunger and poverty."[64] The noted University of Toronto scholar Ursula Franklin has suggested that, when the City of Toronto declared homelessness a disaster, it should have prompted governments to provide emergency shelter, food and clothing in response to this "man-made disaster," as happened in the 1997 Manitoba floods and the 1998 Quebec ice storms.[65] No such initiative, of course, was forthcoming.

Much attention has been directed to the concept of the "feminization of poverty." More emphasis must be placed on the link between women's poverty and homelessness. Economic security is directly related to providing the basics of life, including food, clothing and shelter. Yet economic security has been eroded among low and middle income women over the past decade, Inequality in employment opportunities, working at part-time, semi-skilled jobs, and taking on the double burden of marketplace and domestic work have resulted in women being poorer than men. Approximately half of all unattached females over the age of sixty-five live below the poverty line of $10,233 for single city dwellers and 42 per cent of families headed by women live below the poverty line of $20,812 for an urban family of four.[66] Women are economically marginalized by low-wage jobs and lack the economic security of a guaranteed standard of living that would permit enhanced participation economically, politically and culturally in their communities. The result is that women have not shown progress in achieving economic equality, First Nations people endure appalling living conditions and one and a half million Canadian children live in poverty.[67]

## The Effects of Women's Homelessness

The majority of women in this study stated that a lack of money and unemployment were the primary reasons for their homelessness. In discussing the effects of poverty on their lives, they stressed themes of hunger, poor health, educational restrictions and an inability to "get ahead." Many suggested that they had difficulty finding rental accommodation to correspond with the meager amount of money available to them. They spoke of making choices among paying rent, buying food or purchasing clothing, since it was not possible for them to stretch their limited funds to take care of all their needs. All were vulnerable to homelessness and, indeed, became homeless when a precipitating incident occurred such as the loss of a job, removal from the welfare rolls or a decrease in welfare payments. Eleven women found shelter with friends or relatives, preferring such arrangements to residing in a hostel, particularly if they had children; the remainder were left on the streets.

Judy is a thirty-five-year-old Caucasian woman who described herself as "having it all" until she lost her banking job in a restructuring initiative. When her marriage ended a year later, she turned to alcohol for comfort. "That's when things really went down hill, but I clean up real good especially if I am going on a job interview." The "middle class slip" applies to more than her appearance, since Judy would rather "live in a hole-in-the-wall near Rosedale than have a Parkdale address." She prefers to purchase presentable clothing from the Salvation Army in order to have a telephone and the "luxury" of reading a daily newspaper, hoping her efforts will lead to another "big ticket" job in the future.

The strengths of many of the women that emerged in these interviews centred on their resourcefulness, concern for their children, desire for security and daily survival skills in stretching funds, finding hand-outs, "making do" and recycling. Most took a rugged individualist approach based on the will to survive; many were self-reliant and oriented to problem solving. Jill worked as a part-time cashier but lost her job at the same time as she sustained a spinal injury. When her husband also lost his janitorial job, she found the bills piling up and the couple could no longer afford their apartment rent. Unable to find cheaper accommodations, she moved her family of five into the small crowded home of a friend. "I was trapped between different needs such as cutting back on food to buy winter coats and boots for the kids. It's rough because the kids eat a lot of macaroni and cheese rather than meat and fresh fruit." She was eventually able to obtain welfare and move into a townhouse for a year. After six months of residency, the monthly rent was raised from $650 to $735. From there, she went to a family shelter.

When low-income women are estranged from their families and lack social support (including dependable and affordable childcare), another picture emerges. Due to ongoing disputes with her parents, Janie and her two-year-old daughter had to leave home before she was able to establish herself financially. When she attempted to set up her own apartment, a decrease in welfare payments made it impossible for her to maintain that home. The lack of affordable daycare resulted in her being unable to look for employment. She lived with a friend for a few months but, when that relationship ended, she temporarily placed her child with the Children's Aid Society and took up residency in a shelter. She then faced the difficulty of finding a job with no permanent address, no telephone and no place to clean her clothing.

A 1998 United Way of Greater Toronto report entitled *Freedom From Violence: A Case for Increased Support for Abused Women* cited a decrease in core funding and related community service directed to women escaping from violence in personal relations. Approximately 8,450 women and children sought refuge in 1996 in shelter and hostel accommodation due to domestic violence; 75 percent of these women had children under the age of five years. United Way president, Ann Golden, has suggested that "poverty and housing are fundamental issues for abused women and their children," attributing the responsibility for a decrease in service to the provincial government.[68] Abuse and the subsequent loss of their homes underline a set of precipitating factors for home-lessness among a substantial number of women in this study. Young women described physical and sexual victimization; middle-age women were more likely to report physical abuse in marital and common-law relationships.

The process of becoming homeless involved a series of interlocking factors for Sandra, a resident of one of the cheap motels operated by Scarborough West Social Services. The connection among battering, family disruption, poverty and homelessness was established early in her life when she was beaten by her father and forced to leave home in her early teens. Lacking a high school diploma, she discovered that she could not even find work at a fast food outlet. Years later, she was again forced to flee from her home when her husband also became abusive. Without relatives in the city to whom she could turn for support, she felt it necessary to reconcile with her husband. She "hit rock bottom" when he beat her so badly that her jaw was broken in two places and she lost two of her upper front teeth. She ended her mar-riage, managed to survive for some time on little money and through precarious living arrangements, and finally decided to apply for welfare. Homelessness was her adaptive response to battering; violence forced her back into pover-ty and homelessness.

A substantial number of homeless women cited poor health as a primary cause of their difficulties. Medical com-plaints ranged from respiratory infections, asthma, diabetes, cancer, as well as HIV infections and AIDS. Community health centres are overwhelmed with women that have been discharged from under-funded hospitals without adequate treatment protocols. Sally, a slim, attractive Caucasian woman, dropped out of school at age seventeen, taking to the streets to panhandle for a living. Due to her age, she did not qualify for welfare; her pregnant condition and the fact that she had a child living with her mother made her ineligible for mother's allowance. Hospitalized with Lupus and several other physical ailments, her subsequent release into homelessness (at a time when she was attempting to find work) resulted in setting aside her plans out of fear that her illnesses would not allow her to be independent and live outside a hospital.

According to the Mayor's Action Task Force on Homelessness, shelter data reveals a profile of some 170,000 individuals who were homeless in the City of Toronto during 1996. One-third of the homeless had difficulties stemming from mental illness and a large percentage of that population had concurrent abuse disorders.[69] Barbara, a thirty-eight-year-old Caucasian woman, lost her part-time job at a bakery with the onset of symptoms associated with her psychological disability. At the same time as her public assistance benefits were cut by almost 22 per cent, she lost the support of her family and custody of her twelve-year-old daughter to her ex-husband. She lives in an illegal, unheated basement apartment that was scheduled for demolition. On any given day she may unable to think clearly or to function adequately. After years of being in and out of hospital diagnosed with schizophrenia, she refuses to take her medications of Haldol, Loxapac, Clozapine and Risperidone in view of the debilitating side effects (including involuntary facial movements, grimacing and an inability to read). Lately, she reports feeling suicidal, contemplating ending her problems by stepping in front of a subway train.

For some women, death emphasizes how limited the

social efforts are to find a permanent solution to homelessness. The Toronto Coalition Against Homelessness in 1997
reported that death due to homelessness of women was less
publicized than for men. There are approximately three to
four deaths among the homeless each week in Toronto,
according to Cathy Crowe, street nurse with Queen Street
West Community Health Center. She observes that deaths
are not often attributed to homelessness because individuals
die as a result of health problems and substance abuse.
Nonetheless, some 55 percent of street deaths are attributed
to illness such as exposure and hypothermia related to being
homeless.[70]

Barbara's case is illustrative of one of the most pressing
issues of systemic discrimination for women with psychiatric
disabilities. Recent changes in provincial government policies
resulted in deinstitutionalization, while the much vaunted
community support failed to materialize.[71] A strategy to
introduce a widespread, easily accessible and affordable network of community services was undertaken by the NDP
government in 1993 to replace large impersonal institutions
with more humane community living arrangements.[72] More
recently, due to lack of funding, many patients were discharged without proper needs assessments, and women
whose difficulties stemmed from mental illness were accom-
modated in hostels, jails and on the street.

Approximately half of the women in this study used
alcohol and drugs; a number were suffering from health
problems due to addiction. Many of the older women on the
streets prefer alcohol, while young women living in a similar
manner are likely to use crack cocaine. Betty will sleep in
one of three spots in Riverdale park during the summer and
in shelters during the winter in order to be able to afford a
small bottle of wine with which she puts herself to sleep
most evenings. When she began using heroin in the early
1990s, Gillian was a wife and mother, a gymnastics coach and

a Sunshine Girl for the *Toronto Sun*. Unaware that "it would grab hold of my life," she thought heroin was the "cool and trendy thing to do" with her friends. As her addiction progressed she gave up coaching. When she separated from her husband, Gillian moved about the city prostituting. "Now that I'm clean, I wonder how I could do that, but it's the easiest twenty dollars you can make." Forced to send her sons to their aunt's home for care was described as "the worst feeling in the world; when you lose your children, what is there left?" She credited the support she received from the Adelaide Drop-In Center for Women with turning her life around upon completing a methadone program at The Meeting Place. "Funny, the things you miss," she stated. "We are forced to beg, scrape or steal to survive. Little things like television, cable, telephones or little comforts that other people take for granted are luxuries for us."

According to Rodney Elie of the Anishnawabe Health Patrol, 25 per cent of those on the streets are Aboriginal, although they comprise only 2 per cent of the city's population.[73] There is a disproportionate number of Native women among the homeless. Forty-one-year-old Vivian is one of them. Together with her husband Len, she has occupied a doorway of an abandoned building for the past three years. Vivian grew up on a Mohawk reserve in northern Ontario; Len was raised a few blocks from their doorway on Queen Street. Both suffer health problems related to chronic alcoholism. The doorway in which they reside is very small with just enough room for two people to sit, but not enough for either to stretch out to sleep. It is insulated with double mattresses and a bevy of blankets as a top cover. Privacy is afforded by a blanket that hangs across the front door. Both Vivian and Len insist that visitors ought to recognize this as a home and appropriately knock to the side of the blanket rather than merely whisking it aside to see if they are "home."

The intersection of race, class and gender argues for the way in which multi-layered subordination is socially constructed in Rachael's life. A forty-five-year old Black Canadian woman, she was only one of two Black and one South Asian woman found in shelters and drop-in centres in this study. While she currently shares an apartment with her husband, in the past she joined men, women and children in soup-kitchen lines when she lived on the street for five years. Her few recreational breaks are taken at Sistering, the community based , drop-in center where she meets many of the "regulars" who are her friends. A very articulate and intelligent woman, she is quick to point out that she has been denied access to housing and employment because of her race, but equally quick to say that she tries not to let that "interfere with taking control of [her] life." She readily admits spending "too much money on drugs" (a habit she has successfully eliminated) instead of saving it for her eighteen-year-old son.

She summarizes the reasons for her difficulties including inadequate income, shortage of affordable housing, decrease in social support, fear of landlords, difficulties concerning race relations with neighbours and problems of substance abuse and health. Subsequent to her husband's accident on a construction site that left him a paraplegic, she has devoted most of her time to caring for his needs. With a recent increase in her monthly rent to $750, she worries that the combined family income from welfare and disability benefits will not be sufficient to cover living costs. She anticipates beginning to look for less expensive accommodation, hoping in her search not to encounter "racist landlords who smile in your face, but don't want to rent to Blacks."

Elderly women are homeless primarily because they lack adequate income and do not have access to affordable housing and support systems. Studies have identified several potential risk factors for older women's homelessness including structural forces (e.g. housing and job market conditions), living alone, low socioeconomic and occupational status, poor physical and mental health, limited social networks and personal crises.[74] Lillian, a bright and articulate woman, is dressed in a black sheath dress with an obligatory strand of white pearls, symbols of a bygone era of elegance. As a former school teacher, she easily slips into discussing statistics and theories concerning the decline of the middle class in Canada. Influenced by friends and family members into signing over control of her finances, Lillian became convinced that she was no longer capable of managing her affairs. Unable to consistently pay her escalating rent when her funds were depleted, she found the door to her apartment padlocked one day with her belongings placed in boxes near the garbage chute. She is currently sleeping in one of the few women-only shelters until she can secure a room of her own through public-assisted housing.

Many young women interviewed in this survey had previously worked in casual and short-term employment including waitress, babysitter, factory worker, cashier, courier and beauty salon attendant. Their employment seldom paid a living wage that would allow them to secure the basic necessities of food, clothing and shelter. According to a counsellor at Stop 86, young people comprise a quarter of the people living on the streets and in shelters. Many of these young homeless women lack education and related work skills. The focus of the program is on maintaining their pre-employment training as well as providing literacy, life skills programs and vocational counselling. "The shelters are full," Sarah complained. On any given day, she may stop at Shout or Youth Link Inner City if she is looking for a "place to clean up," move on to a church to "grab a snack" and "crash" by late afternoon in a park. In and out of foster care most of her life, her school work went "down hill," resulting in her obtaining a grade ten education. Although she would like to go to college some day, these plans seem removed from the reality of currently living on the streets. While she admitted that she is "a bit lazy and smokes a little dope," she does not see herself as "a bad kid," and hopes that "somebody will give me a chance to prove that I am a good worker."

According to a Covenant House case worker, refugees constitute about one third of the population of the city's shelters and approximately 50 percent of those in shelters that service families. The majority of women who arrive in Canada are sponsored immigrants and the sponsors are usually husbands. Immigrant and refugee women experience isolation, language and cultural barriers, limited job skills and racism that is often compounded by problems of abuse. Tesi is a resident of a Toronto shelter and the only surviving member of her family from the most recent civil war in Angola. At age nineteen she witnessed the murder of her father and siblings, only to view her mother and younger sister die of dysentery in a refugee camp. Despite the enormous tragedy, this intelligent, feisty and determined woman is resolved to continue her education in order to obtain her high school credentials. She is currently studying math, science and English at a local high school and scouring the city to find suitable work and accommodation in anticipation of leaving the shelter. She requires little support and will not entertain pity. There appears to be little doubt that Tesi will make a successful adjustment to her new life and a fine Canadian citizen.

## Strategies of Intervention

A broad public consensus is needed that homelessness in unacceptable in a country as rich as Canada. Public pressure will be required to place the issue of housing back on the agenda as a fundamental human right. Reinvesting in public infrastructure, creating jobs and lowering interest rates are preconditions for addressing abject poverty in Canada.[75] The complex needs of the heterogeneous population of homeless women suggest that housing, social and economic policies must address long-term as well as emergency concerns. The efforts of the City of Toronto have almost exclusively focused on expanding existing hostels, a commendable action but not a long-term solution. Moreover, responsibility must extend to the federal and provincial governments since both can justly be blamed for abandoning social housing. Although homelessness will not be eliminated simply by building more affordable and accessible housing units, it is a critical component of a long-term approach to the problem.

On the historic day of October 29, 1999, the City of Toronto Council passed a motion declaring homelessness to be a "national disaster." Also endorsed were recommendations from 300 organizations and 700 individuals – The Toronto Disaster Relief Committee – that went a long way toward providing appropriate methods to correct the problem. First, it called for immediate, short-term rescue measures for the homeless such as the use of mobile homes, tents and bath houses in city parks, opening emergency infirmaries and increasing funds for community agencies that provide food, shelter and counselling services. Second, it urged that *all* levels of government recognize the problem by declaring it a national disaster. Third, the Committee advised that social services be restored for the homeless, including the reinstatement of adequate social assistance benefits and the conversion of public buildings into emergency shelters. The long-range fiscal goal of this organization is the introduction of the "1% solution," the addition of one percent to government budgets for the purpose of constructing housing to accommodate low-income people.

While there is no single solution to the myriad problems which homelessness creates, with political will there is no shortage of practical suggestions for action to defeat home-

lessness. The Golden Report stresses the need to take steps
to preserve affordable housing, protect and rehabilitate existing homes and construct new low cost apartments and town-
houses. The report states that it is essential to assist those in
danger of losing their homes in order to prevent them from
joining the ranks of the homeless. Over the next five years,
Toronto may lose 25,000 to 50,000 low rent apartments
annually. Between 15,000 and 30,000 new households could
face problems of housing affordability in addition to the
106,000 households that currently experience such difficulties.[76] The key to prevention is to ensure that individuals and
families have adequate income to pay for housing. To this
end, the report calls for $230 million a year from the
province to increase shelter allowances for people on welfare
and a similar program for low income, working families to
ensure that they do not lose their homes. The Golden Report
also favours advocacy for a national housing policy (jointly
coordinated by the federal and provincial governments) to
overcome the "jurisdictional gridlock" that now confounds
(or serves as a convenient excuse to avoid) positive action.

In the Interim Report of the Mayor's Homeless Action
Task Force, nine general strategies to combat homelessness
are put forth including the provision of adequate rental assistance, a separate and distinct strategy for Aboriginal people
and special attention directed toward the 30,000 children
who are waiting for subsidized housing. Some of the one
hundred recommendations of the final report suggest a new
housing development strategy to increase affordable rental
housing by 2,000 units a year. Specific initiatives suggest sub-
sidizing land costs, waiving fees and (sales, goods and service) taxes, modifying property taxes, providing rental supplements and assisting with the cost of mortgage insurance and
capital grants. The report also recommends that the federal
government expand funding for residential rehabilitation and
extend such programs to include rooming houses and suites

in private homes. Encouraging the province to increase shelter allowances for welfare recipients and calling upon the city
of Toronto to establish a $10 million dollar fund for new
housing and rent supplements are key recommendations to
address homelessness in Toronto.

Such initiatives would benefit from creative innovations
and flexibility in planning. It must be recognized that the
complex problem of homelessness has its roots in multiple
economic and political issues, cultural values, family interac-
tions and personal concerns. Underlying concerns of poverty and personal factors of spousal abuse, mental illness and
addiction must also be incorporated into a comprehensive
plan to deal with the provision of housing for economically
vulnerable women. Specific programs addressed to diverse
constituencies including the young, the elderly, Native peo-
ples, refugees, people with physical and mental health problems, addicts, victims of violence and so on would have a far
greater chance of success than current homogenous policies.

As important as persuading the public to press politicians
for genuine reform is the task of altering the perceptions of
the homeless themselves. As Marcuse's work on oppression
and approaches to libertarian housing suggests, homelessness
inhibits protest and undermines resistance, subtly producing
acceptance of conformity and making inadequacy tolerable.[77]
Economic inequality not only affects the health and well-
being of the poor but societies with greater inequality show
signs of social deterioration, the precursors of illness and
decay. At the federal level, a national strategy is needed to
provide additional resources for the building of non-profit
public housing, coordinating the work of the Canadian
Mortgage and Housing Corporation, the Canadian
Federation of Municipalities and the provincial governments.
Belgium levied a tax against uninhabited houses. France
established an ambitious program of building houses for the
disadvantaged. Finland has organized a multifaceted response

of home building, social welfare and health care services, reducing the number of homeless by 50 per cent in ten years.[78] Enshrining the right to housing as has happened in Belgium, Finland, the Netherlands, Portugal and Spain would mean a commitment to a massive home building and a maintenance program for public housing stocks.

Achieving the task of alleviating homelessness will be difficult. Powerful corporate interests, a dominant neoliberal ideology and entrenched social ideas are arrayed against it. The poor in Canada are growing in numbers and the numbers of poor women and children are expanding most of all. There can be no solution to homelessness that does not include the specific concerns of women and children. Even though the incidence of poverty among women is not a new phenomenon, society has not taken steps to address poverty as a woman's issue. Given that the lowest paid, least skilled and most insecure jobs are assigned to women through socialization, and they remain in job ghettos and engage in double duty through public and private sphere work, women are more vulnerable to economic related problems such as homelessness. In locating the structural roots of poverty within unequal access to resources, attention is focused on the enormous and widening gulf between rich and poor, women and men, white people and people of colour and increasingly between the elderly and youth. Mobilizing around poor women, abused women, women struggling to raise children and women who are homeless is critical to provide the economic security necessary to allow women full participation in their society. To accomplish the goals of eradicating women's homelessness, the level of awareness about women's subordination must be raised through popular culture, the media and both formal and informal education. The consequences of inequity in terms of homelessness, health, burden of work, poverty, self-esteem and mortality of women and children is at stake, along with the concomitant problems that ensue. The general public and local organizations working with homeless people must pressure governments to develop the political will required to bring about a resolution of the social problems of women's poverty, abuse and homelessness.

## Notes

This chapter is a much condensed version of a research project by the author and Nir Baraket, Professor of Photography at George Brown College in Toronto. The associated photographic exhibition, together with the full narrative, have won support from numerous agencies such as the United Way of Greater Toronto, that led to several spin-off projects providing help to the homeless, and stimulated critical thinking among many individuals and groups in the Toronto area.

1. P. Goering, D. Paduchak and J. Durbin, "Housing Homeless Women: A Consumer Preference Study," *Hospital and Community Psychiatry*, Vol. 41 (1990), pp. 790-794.

2. Joan Morris, "Affiliation, Gender and Parental Status among Homeless Persons," *Journal of Social Psychology*, Vol. 138 (1998), p. 241.

3. Mary Boes and Katharine van Wormer, "Social Work with Homeless Women in Emergency Rooms: A Strength-Feminist Perspective," *Affilia*, Vol. 12 (Winter, 1997), p. 408.

4. C. Grisby, D. Baumann, S. E. Gregorich and C. Roberts-Gray, "Disaffection to Entrenchment: A Model for Understanding Homelessness," *Journal of Social Issues*, Vol. 46 (1990), pp. 141-156.

5. C. Parker and S. Brown, "Housing and Adult Health: Results of a Lifestyle Study in Worcester, England," *Journal of Epidemiology and Community Health*, Vol. 48 (1994), pp. 555-559.

6. R. Rosenthal, *Homeless in Paradise* (Philadelphia: Temple University Press, 1994).

7. E. Liebow, *Tell Them Who I Am: The Lives of Homeless Women* (New York: Free Press, 1993).

8. Stanley Battle, "Homeless Women and Children: The Question of Poverty," *Child and Youth Services*, Vol. 14 (July, 1990), pp. 111-127; E. Mulroy and T. Lane, "Housing Affordability, Stress and Single Mothers: Pathways to Homelessness," *Journal of Sociology and Social Welfare*, Vol. 19 (1992), pp. 51-64.

9. Boes and van Wormer, *op. cit.*, p. 409.

10. L. Goodman, "The Prevalence of Abuse Among Homeless and Housed Mothers: A Comparative Study," *American Journal of Orthopsychiatry*, Vol. 6 (1991), pp. 489-500.

11. S. Anderson, T. Boe and S. Smith, "Homeless Women," *Afflia*, Vol. 3 (1988), pp. 62-70

12. Bob Olsen, "Global Factors for Homelessness," bobolsen @arcos.org, (1997), p. 1-2.

13. A. Johnson, "Homelessness," *Encyclopedia of Social Work*, 19th edition, Vol. 2 (1995), pp. 1338-1346.

14. P. Koegel, E. Melamiel and M. Burman, "Childhood Risk Factors for Homelessness among Homeless Adults," *American Journal of Public Health*, Vol. 85 (1995), pp. 1649-1659.

15. Boes and van Wormer, *op. cit.*, p. 409.

16. S. Keigher and F. Pratt, "Housing Emergencies and the Etiology of Homelessness among the Elderly," in S. Keigher, ed., *Housing Risks and Homelessness Among the Urban Elderly* (New York: Haworth Press, 1991).

17. Thomas Hirschl and Mark Rank, "The Likelihood of Poverty Across the American Life Span," *Social Work*, Vol. 2 (1999), pp. 24-32.

18. Toronto Drop-in Coalition, "Breaking the Fall: The Role of Drop-ins from the Perspective of Those Who Use Them," Toronto (1997).

19. National Council on Welfare, "Child Poverty in Canada," (Ottawa: 1997).

20. City of Toronto, "Terms of Reference for the Homelessness Action Task Force," (January, 1998).

21. Andrew Jackson, David Robinson, Bob Baldwin and Cindy Wiggins, *Falling Behind: The State of Working Canada* (Ottawa: Canadian Centre for Policy Alternatives, 2000), pp. 85-94.

22. Canadian Council on Social Development, "Progress of Canada's Children" (Ottawa, 1996), p. 32.

23. City of Toronto Department of Public Health, "Community Harm Reduction Strategies for Homeless People During Severe Weather," Toronto, (March, 1996).

24. Ontario Coalition Against Poverty, "Who's Cheating Who? An Inquiry into the Abuse of the Poor by the Welfare System," (Toronto, 1997), p. 1.

25. Not coincidentally, the British *Poor Law Amendment* Act of 1834 and various laws (e.g., the *Municipal Reform Act* of 1835) extending powers to create constabularies passed almost simultaneously, as English authorities confronted working class radicals who

had operated in various forms for over twenty years. In the shadow of the middle class victory, the Great Reform Bill of 1832, came the *Poor Law* of 1834 which split the "working poor" from "workhouse paupers," condemning the latter to official workhouses, known as "bastilles." See Victor Bailey, "The Fabrication of Deviance: 'Dangerous Classes' and 'Criminal Classes' in Victorian England," in John Rule and Robert Malcolmson, eds., *Protest and Survival: Essays for E. P. Thompson* (London: Merlin Press, 1993), pp. 221-256. Unlike contemporary neoliberals, the English authorities at least were honest about their intentions. Their explicit goal, according to officials, was "to make the workhouses as much like prisons as possible [and] to establish therein a discipline so severe and repulsive as to make them a terror to the poor and prevent them from entering." Quoted in E. P. Thompson, *The Making of the English Working Class* (Harmondsworth: Penguin, 1968), p. 295.

26. Ann Slavinsky and Ann Cousins, "Homeless Women," *Nursing Outlook,* Vol. 30 (1992), pp. 358-362. For a fuller analysis of the way in which governments, corporations and the media depict the poor and distort the causes of poverty, see Jean Swanson, *Poor Bashing* (Toronto: Between the Lines, 2001).

27. Tish Durkin, "Poverty Is Your Problem," *Madamoiselle* (September, 1996), pp. 58-61.

28. S. Cox, "Daily Bread Food Bank Marks 15 Years," *The Toronto Star* (24 February, 1999), p. A-14.

29. The phrase "Toronto the Good" was around for some time prior to being used by C. S. Clark in his book *Of Toronto the Good: The Queen City of Canada as It Is* (Montreal: Toronto Publishing Company, 1898), reprinted in 1978 (Toronto: Coles). According to Clark, the city was championed in this manner at the Social Purity Congress of 1896 in Baltimore and the World's Convention of the Women's Christian Temperance Union held in Toronto in 1897. Edward Mann took up this characterization ironically when he discussed the difficulties encountered by some Torontonians living in poverty. See: W. E. Mann, *The Underside of Toronto* (Toronto: McClelland and Stewart, 1970).

30. The Mayor's Action Task Force on Homelessness, "Breaking the Cycle of Homelessness: The Interim Report," City of Toronto (July, 1999).

31. Andrew Jackson, David Robinson, Bob Baldwin and Cindy Wiggins, *Falling Behind: The State of Working Canada, 2000* (Ottawa: Canadian Centre for Policy Alternatives, 2000), p. 117.

32. *Ibid.*, p. 122.

33. E. Carey, "A Province of 'Haves and Have Nots'," *The Toronto Star* (13 November, 1998), p. A-4.

34. R. Spears, "Deficit War Won on Backs of Unemployed," *The Toronto Star* (9 June, 1998), p. A-19.

35. V. Lawton, "Canada 'Neglecting' Jobless," *The Toronto Star* (17 October, 1998), p. A-6.

36. John Honderich, "Heartening Response to Homelessness" [editorial] *The Toronto Star* (10 October, 1998), p. A-22.

37. John Honderich, "No Pal of the Homeless," [editorial] *The Toronto Star* (14 January, 1999), p. A-20.

38. Ian Urquhart, "Eves Wants Property Tax Bill Cut for Businesses," *The Toronto Star* (21 October, 1998), p. A-4.

39. Social Planning Council of Metropolitan Toronto, "Who Does What to Whom," *SPC Sound Bite,* Vol. 1 (October, 1997), pp. 1-9.

40. Dan Anstett, "The Experiences of Homeless Families in Toronto in 1997," unpublished Master of Social Work thesis, York University, Toronto (September, 1997).

41. The increase in cost for the City of Toronto's public housing is $269 million. The backlog on repairs for Ontario's 84,000 neglected public housing units was estimated in 1994 to be $230 million, to which the province contributed $42 million in 1997. See Nicole Sequin, "Tories are Destroying Housing," *The Toronto Star* (24 August, 1998), p. A-17.

42. Ontario Non-Profit Housing Association and the Co-operative Housing Federation of Canada, "Where's Home? A Picture of Housing Needs in Ontario," Ottawa (1999).

43. Ibid., p. 8.

44. Paul Moloney, "Rental Shortage Compared to the 40s," *The Toronto Star* (3 May, 1999), p. B-3.

45. Public Housing Inquiry, "Province-Wide Consultation on the Future of Public Housing: Final Report and Recommendations," (Toronto: April, 1998).

46. C. Dunphy, "National Summit on Homelessness," *The Toronto Star* (8 February, 1999, p.A-1.

47. I. Urquhart, "Golden Report Challenges Opposition," *The Toronto Star* (19 January, 1999), p.A-15.

48. C. Vaughan, "A History Lesson on Homelessness," *The Toronto Star* (12 October, 1998), p. A-8.

49. Ontario Non-Profit Housing Association and the Co-operative Housing Federation of Canada, "Household Payment of Rent as Function of Income," Ottawa (1999), p. 18.

50. Ibid., p. 22.

51. Homeless Action Task Force, "Background Paper for the Homeless Action Task Force," City of Toronto, January, 1998.

52. E. Carey, "Family Income Plays 'Crucial Role'," *The Toronto Star* (8 May, 1999), p. E-5.

53. Jack Lakey, "Campaign Gives Homeless a Voice," *The Toronto Star* (8 October, 1998), p. A-7

54. Mayor's Homelessness Action Task Force, *op. cit.*, p. 27.

55. Laura Butterbaugh, "Homelessness: Women Search for Answers," *Off Our Backs*, Vol. 28 (July, 1998), pp. 12-14.

56. Mayor's Homelessness Action Task Force, *op. cit.*, p. 17. It is worth noting some comparative statistics. The proportion of children in families with incomes less than 50 per cent of the median in the U.S.A. is 24 per cent. Canada has only about half as many children in relative poverty with 12 per cent living with less than half the median income. In the United Kingdom, however, the proportion drops almost by half again to 7.5 per cent, and, in both Germany and Sweden, the number goes down to 4 per cent. By this measure of equity, only the record of the United States is significantly worse than Canada's among developed countries. See Jackson et al., *op. cit.*, p. 131.

57. The United Nations Covenant, adopted in 1966, guaranteed the right to adequate food, clothing, housing, health care, education and other rights contained in the Universal Declaration of Human Rights. As a signatory, Canada pledged to respect the rights of its citizens to these entitlements. Canada is plainly in violation of the fundamental right to an adequate standard of living including food, clothing and housing.

58. Valerie Lawton, "Claims Dropped in the Two Years After the Program Changed," *The Toronto Star* (19 March, 1999), p. A-20.

59. Valerie Lawton, "Liberals Using Quotas to Trim UI Rolls: NDP," *The Toronto Star* (4 February, 1999), p. A-6.

60. Helen Branswell, "Canadians Wouldn't Give Answers on Poverty, UN Officials Say," *The National Post* (November 8, 1998), p. A-4. Age is an important factor in the social construction of poverty and it is becoming more important. In 1980, 47 per cent of young people under 24 were living below the official poverty line; by 1997, that figure had risen to 61 per cent. Similarly, in 1980, 23 per cent of Canadians between 24 and 35 lived in poverty; by 1997, that too had risen to 31%. As discomfiting as these data are, however, "the greatest burden on poverty falls on women, whether as single women, women in families, or as single parent women. 56 per cent of single parent women live in poverty." See Jackson et al., *op. cit.*, p. 135.

61. NAWL, "National Association of Women and the Law Report on Women and Poverty," (Ottawa: NAWL, 1998), p. 8.

62. *Ibid.*, p. 14.

63. Caroline Mallan, "Tories Focus on Welfare Reform," *The Toronto Star* (30 April, 1999), p. 14.

64. Michelle Landsburg, "Harris Shrugs off Responsibility," *The Toronto Star* (8 October, 1998), p. A-7.

65. Lakey, *loc. cit.*

66. Anon., "The House that Joy Built: Downtrodden Women Find a Haven Downtown," (Toronto: 416 Drop-in Centre, 1998), p. 1.

67. Branswell, *op. cit.*, p.A-4.

68. The United Way of Greater Toronto, "Freedom from Violence: A Case for Increased Support for Abused Women," Toronto (1998), pp. 34-38.

69. Mayor's Homeless Action Task Force, *op. cit.*, p. 45.

70. Personal interview, 4 January, 1999.

71. Toronto Coalition Against Homelessness, "Toronto Coalition Against Homelessness Responds One Year Later: Our Verdict," Toronto (May, 1997).

72. Community Information Centre of Metropolitan Toronto, "Emptying the Mental Hospitals: The Deinstitutionalization of People with Mental Health Problems," Toronto (1998), p. 3.

73. Personal interview, 2 April, 1999.

74. E. Susser, E. Struening and S. Conover, "Psychiatric Problems in Homeless Men," *Archives of General Psychiatry*, Vol. 48 (1989), pp. 848-856.

75. See the work of Armine Yalnizyan, economist and social policy consultant of the Centre for Social Justice, entitled "Poverty in Canada," Ottawa, (1999).

76. Mayor's Homeless Action Task Force, *op. cit.*, pp. 4-7.

77. See P. Marcuse, "The Other Side of Housing: Oppression and Liberation," in B. Turner, ed., *Between State and Market: Housing in the Post-Industrial Era* (Philadelphia: Coronet, 1987).

78. Philip Alston, "Hardship in the Midst of Plenty," in *Progress of Nations: The Nations of the World Ranked According to Their Achievements in Fulfillment of Child Rights and Progress for Women* (New York: United Nations, 1998), p.31.

# Arthur Kroker
# and the Canadian Mind

## Howard A. Doughty

If Canadians have demonstrated any extraordinary capacity to contribute to modern culture, our singular gift is arguably best found in the domain of social communication – its practice in the popular arts and entertainment, its facilitation by means of technological innovation, and its interpretation by philosophers and commentators especially concerned with the impact of mass communication on our daily lives. It is generally agreed that Canadians added only marginally to the lasting stock of nineteenth-century prose and poetry in English. By contrast, there have been plenty of twentieth-century *literati* of sufficient stature and with enough Booker prizes and nominations to make up at least in part for past provincialism. The ledger includes such entries as Milton Acorn, Margaret Atwood, the pre-adolescent Saul Bellow, Earle Birney, Neil Bissoondath, Christian Bök, Morley and Barry Callaghan, Austin Clarke, Leonard Cohen, Matt Cohen, Robertson Davies, Marion Engel, Timothy Findley, Dave Godfrey, Robert Kroetsch, Irving Layton, the post-adolescent Stephen Leacock, Hugh MacLennan, Margaret Laurence, Malcolm Lowry however briefly, Yann Martel, Rohinton Mistry, W.O. Mitchell, Brian Moore, Farley Mowat, Alice Munro, Susan Musgrave, Michael Ondaatje, Al Purdy, Mordechai Richler, Rick Salutin, F.R. Scott, Carol Shields, Clara Thomas, Jane Urquhart, Miriam Waddington, Rudy Wiebe, and dozens more. It has nonetheless been on the stage, in motion pictures and on television that Canadian stars have most brightly shone. So, when compelled to admit that ice hockey games between Anaheim and Tampa Bay no longer stir the great, white northern soul, Canadians can amuse themselves by constructing whiggish historical rosters of popular entertainers who left (sometimes for good) their homes and/or native land to gain international (i.e., American) approval and to become statistically over-represented in the shimmering skies of the U.S. cultural night.[1]

## Canadian Performers, Directors and Producers

Such catalogues commonly include "America's Sweetheart" Mary Pickford (alias Gladys Mary Smith of Toronto), Fay (*King Kong*) Wray, William Henry Pratt (a.k.a. Boris Karloff, at least a temporary Canadian and an actor who scared the pants off moviegoers) and Louis B. Mayer (a Hollywood mogul from New Brunswick who scared the pants off movie actors), Norman Jewison, Ted Kotcheff, Atom Egoyan and David Cronenberg (a movie producer who scares off more than pants). They feature a number of leading males and occasional leading females from Raymond Massey, Walter Pidgeon, Norma Shearer, Hume Cronyn, Rod Cameron, Lorne Greene, Glenn Ford, Raymond Burr, Alexis Smith, and Deanna Durbin, to Leslie Neilsen, William Shatner, and Genevieve Bujold. They also feature domestic leads and Hollywood supporting actors Lloyd Bochner, Donnelly Rhodes, Sara Botsford, John Vernon and Al Waxman. They certainly must include Walter Huston. They would surely accommodate Christopher Plummer and Donald Sutherland and might even make room for Sutherland scion Keefer, the elusive Margot Kidder, Michael Sarrazin and Jay Silverheels (originally Harold J. Smith and more famously "Tonto"), *Homicide: Life on the Street*'s Clark Johnson, *Law and Order* prosecutor, Jackie Kennedy impersonator and *Crossing Jordan* medical examiner

Jill Hennessy, TV shock show host Jenny Jones, *Due South*'s
Paul Gross, *JAG*'s David James Elliott, *Sex and the City*'s Kim
Cattrall and the cast of *Women Fully Clothed,* Nero Wolfe's
most recent incarnation in the substantial form of Maury
Chevkin, the estimable Graham Greene, the admirable Kate
Nelligan, the worthy Brent Carver, the exemplary Tom
Jackson, the Baywatched Pamela Anderson (Lee?), the short-
lived *Max Bickford*'s TV transsexual Helen Shaver and *The
Quiet American* Brendan Fraser. The list goes on.

Like gifted actors from John Drainie to Gordon Pinsent,
Bruno Gerussi, Eric Peterson, Sonja Smits, Albert Schultz, the
Dale girls, and R.H. Thomson, news and public affairs special-
ists have – despite plenty of opportunities to head south –
mainly preferred to tend the home fires; but, notice may still
be taken of Morley Safer, Robert MacNeill, Peter Jennings,
Keith Morrison, Thalia Assuras, John (alias J.D.) Roberts, ex-
*Good Morning America* host and happily repatriated Kevin
Newman, too-honest-for-prime-time Arthur Kent, revolving
talking heads at CNN, and economist-pundit John Kenneth
Galbraith. Likewise radio "personalities" with the memory of
Peter Gzowski standing in for the entire cast and crew of what
has now been re-invented as CBC Radio One, remain singu-
larly definitive of the domestic Canadian soul.

Musicians might be represented by Guy Lombardo, Percy
Faith, Glenn Gould, Maynard Ferguson, Moe Koffman, Oscar
Peterson and, more recently, by "pop-jazz crossover queen"
Diana Krall. Some of Canada's most valued musicians and
singers, including Bruce Cockburn, Wade Hemsworth, Don
Messer, Garnet Rogers, Stan Rogers, and the incomparable
"Stompin' Tom" Conners, have mainly centred their careers
in Canada, but the list of serious and popular international
stars contains Maureen Forrester, Teresa Stratas and Jon
Vickers, country music legend Hank Snow, Giselle
Mackenzie, Robert Goulet (admittedly a transplant from
Massachusetts who made memorable cigarette commercials

and played a stunning Sir Lancelot opposite Richard Burton some forty years ago), *The Four Lads*, *The Crew Cuts*, *The Diamonds*, Paul Anka, one-hit-wonder Bobby Curtola, Ian & Sylvia, Gordon Lightfoot, Joni Mitchell, Anne Murray, Buffy Saint-Marie, *The Mamas and the Papas'* Denny Doherty, *The Lovin' Spoonful's* Zal Yanovsky, *Blood, Sweat & Tears'* David Clayton-Thomas, Neil Young, Burton Cummings and Randy Bachman, most members of *The Band*, *Steppenwolf*, Leonard Cohen (once more), k. d. lang, Kate & Anna McGarrigle and Rufus Wainwright, Bryan Adams, *Barenaked Ladies*, Carole Pope, Shania Twain, Alanis Morisette, Sarah McLachlan, the upstart Avril Lavigne, the ubiquitous Céline "God Bless America" Dion, Jann Arden, Nelly Furtado, Amanda Marshall, Swollen Members, Sum 41, Nickleback and any number of evanescent pop stars of yesterday, today and tomorrow. The list goes relentlessly on.

Nor have the lights of comedians and comic actors dimmed as Canadians from Mack Sennett to Johnny Wayne and Frank Schuster (whose record for most appearances on the *Ed Sullivan Show* can never be broken) through Mort Sahl, Rich Little, David Steinberg, Conrad Bain, Michael J. Fox, Howie Mandel, Leslie Neilsen (again) to Dan Ackroyd, John Candy, Jim Carrey, Tom Cavanagh, the unfathomable Tom Green, Phil Hartman, Eugene Levi, Norm MacDonald, Andrea Martin, Colin Mochrie, Rick Moranis, Mike Myers, Catharine O'Hara, Martin Short, Dave Thomas and all those *Kids in the Hall* made and continue to make Americans laugh and laugh.

Not to be ignored are ex-Ronnie Hawkins side-man and major music producer David Foster, the University of Guelph English teacher who wrote the original *Rambo*, *Superman* creator Joe Shuster (Frank's cousin, who based the fictional *Daily Planet* on the *Toronto Daily Star*), *Saturday Night Live* producer Lorne Michaels, and the motion picture producer who most recently sunk the *Titanic*.

Who knows? There could even be places for David Letterman's side-kick Paul Shaffer, magician and Natural Law Party enthusiast Doug Henning, Hollywood hangers-on Alan Thicke and Suzanne Somers' husband, *Let's Make a Deal* impresario Monty Hall, *Jeopardy*'s Alex Trebek and that darnedest kid of all, Art Linkletter. The list can and does go on and on and tediously on.

## Canadians as Technical Innovators

A modest registry of "firsts" in technological innovation can similarly be developed with neither serious thought nor extensive research. Many Canadians will "know" that the first telephone call was made by Alexander Graham Bell in Brantford, Ontario (despite the fact that Bell immigrated to Canada in 1870 and emigrated to the U.S.A. in 1871, three years before the fabulous first sentence "Watson, come here; I need you").[2] They will also know, on better evidence, that Bell conducted much of his research into disparate areas from aeronautics to hearing aids at his summer home in Baddeck, Nova Scotia, where he expired on 2 August, 1922. They will be reliably informed that Guglielmo Marconi's first trans-Atlantic radio message linked Newfoundland's Signal Hill with Poldhu in Cornwall, England, that Edward S. Rogers invented the "batteryless radio," that the first regularly sched-uled radio station was XWA (now CFCF) in Montreal, that the first continent-wide radio network was put in place by the Canadian National Railway, that, in the days before com-munications satellites such as the pioneering Anik, the world's first regularly scheduled commercial jet aircraft (the North Star) was available to fly the film of the coronation of Queen Elizabeth II to Canada for subsequent television viewing, and that, in 1997, Tim Collins invented the V-chip to leave parents contented that their children would not hear the f-word on television while they merrily surfed swinger-sites on their computers. Now, Canada participates exhaustively in the various electronic media and can claim to be one of the world's most fully "wired" (soon to be "wireless") countries in terms, for example, of cell phones and cable television.

The point? Canadians communicate amply and amusingly among themselves and with others, and have helped devise – no doubt in response to well-known geographic and demographic factors – remarkable means to do so through technologies from snowshoes and birch bark canoes to the snowmobile and (Nortel's twenty-first century corporate mishaps notwithstanding) fibre optics.

## Canadians as Social Critics

What is less well appreciated is the extent to which the Canadian intelligentsia has been instrumental in shaping local and global understanding of what these formidable talents and superior technologies have meant for human communication in the modern and postmodern worlds.

The relative obscurity of Canadian intellectuals may partly be explained as a function of our overall national dopiness. This trait has been frequently, if informally, documented in quizzes in which otherwise functioning citizens – many with certified post-secondary education – can be counted upon to display an appalling ignorance of the most rudimentary facts of science, history and the arts.

The invisibility of our *savants* may also be the result of a perverse pride that many take in the distance between themselves and minimal cultural literacy. William Burrill, shortly before abandoning his post as the "senior writer" of one of Toronto's "alternative" newspapers, *eye*, provided a fine example by ridiculing *Maclean's* magazine's list of "the 100 most important Canadians in history."[3] He apparently found nothing wrong with the concept of such an elitist list, but he disagreed vehemently with the people that *Maclean's* included. Individuals such as William Aberhart, Harold Innis, Cornelius Kreighoff, Louis-Hippolyte LaFontaine, Andre Laurendeau, Henry Morgentaler, O.D. Skelton and Catherine Parr Trail were derisively dismissed as members of a "baffling Who's Who of Who the Hell Are These Guys?"[4] With a couple of exceptions such as World War I flying ace Billy Bishop and astronaut Marc Garneau, Burrill's preferred inventory was composed largely of artists and athletes. I mean no disrespect to the likes of Jean Beliveau, Paul Henderson, Gordie Howe, Fergie Jenkins, Bobby Orr, "Rocket" Richard, Elvis Stojko, and Gilles and Jacques Villeneuve; but, identifying these physically gifted athletes as the best of Canada's best reveals a gap between even *Maclean's* (hardly an overpowering intellectual journal) and the ersatz counter-cultural subsidiary of *The Toronto Star* that is symptomatic of our fixation on professional entertainment as the preferred means to evade serious public issues.

A third problem, however, has more to do with the faults of the communications analysts than with the masses who cheerfully ignore them. One of the few things that newspaper tycoon Roy Thomson and popular writer Pierre Berton could agree on was this: for a communications expert, Marshall McLuhan sure was a lousy communicator. Whether by means of turgid, academic prose or self-indulgently *avant-garde* argot, the propensity of the denizens of the ivory tower of babble to speak in codes for exclusive, self-selected audiences is as unfortunate as it is widespread. Still, in some cases, the struggle to demystify difficult texts is worth the trouble. Especially notable authorities whose analyses of communication and (in the principal cases) the relationship among ideology, technology and global empires are, of course, Burrill's "nobodies" – Harold Innis, Northrop Frye, Marshall McLuhan and George Grant.

It is no accident that each of these theorists can be called "conservative," at least in the sense that they are not uncritically enthralled by the nature of the electronic media and their effects on contemporary society in general and on Canadian society in particular. All were aware of the precarious autonomy of Canada's political economy. Each saw the Canadian experiment as an uncertain contest between the will and imagination of its stubbornly un–American inhabitants and the hegemonic American empire which extended its influence northward as much by cultural as by political, economic and military means. As far as Canadian independence was concerned, their moods were often tinged with melancholy and sometimes with bitterness on those occasions when they were not wholly tragic.

In *The Strategy of Culture* (1952), Innis described the influence of "mechanized communication" originating in the United States as "fatal" for Canada.[5] In *Letters in Canada* (1959), Frye said that this "is practically the only country left in the world which is a pure colony, colonial in psychology and well as in mercantile economics."[6] In *The Bush Garden* (1971), he offered this: "To enter the United States is a matter of crossing an ocean: to enter Canada is a matter of being silently swallowed by an alien continent."[7] McLuhan's expansive, universalistic Catholicism denied him the option of being a nationalist. He had only contempt for the "national question," and embraced the politics of Pierre Trudeau partly because of their common indifference to economics but largely because of their shared hostility to so-called "tribalism." His media studies nonetheless provided much of the groundwork to help others understand and lament the fate of small societies caught up in the maelström of global information technology. George Grant, of course, did not require McLuhan's help in order to fashion his obituary for Canada, *Lament for a Nation* (1965). He wrote: "As Canadians we attempted a ridiculous task in trying to build a conservative nation in the age of progress, on a continent we share with the most dynamic nation on earth."° The engine of this dynamism was technology, first industrial technology and later the technology of communications that insinuated itself into our lives, our living rooms and ultimately our living bodies. Whether or not the Canadian project was doomed from the start, it was the most popular of these sages, Marshall McLuhan, who once advocated the immediate and permanent destruction of all television sets! To this formidable group of scholars, it may be time to add the name of Arthur Kroker. He is hip, he is hyped, and he has some important and possibly profoundly conservative things to say

## Arthur Kroker Is Hip

What other fifty-something Canadian professor of political science publishes dense polysyllabic tomes with accompanying musical CDs to provide the appropriate ambiance for his insights? What other established academic can get away with book subtitles that pledge intellectual explorations of "panic sex" and "electric flesh" only to fulfill that promise with scholarly references to Nietzsche, Heidegger and Baudrillard, interspersed with photographs of tattoos, Christian Dior cosmetics ads, transvestite pornography, garden variety leather bondage and *Penthouse* centrefolds without the staples? What other schoolman would admit to performing in his own "hyper-rock band" called *Sex Without Secretions*, and would publish such a sentence as: "We are data trash and it's good?"[9]

## Arthur Kroker Is Hyped

Arthur Kroker has been publicized as a "Nietzsche for the 90s"; he has been heralded as a "McLuhan for the millennium." Loquacious literary critic John Leonard has praised the "inspired rants" of "Canadian wildman Kroker."[10] His appearances on old television shows such as the CBC Newsworld's *Future World* and the attention paid to him by right-of-mainstream magazines such as the lamentably defunct *Saturday Night* (which entitled its 1996 profile "Geek with an Argument"[11]) demonstrate that his influence is spreading. His celebrity goes far beyond the coteries of obscure and obscurantist "culture critics," who once read his very reputable professional publication *The Canadian Journal of Political and Social Theory* in the late 1970s and 1980s. That journal, it might be recalled, boasted articles by Canadian and international authors of such impressive stature and wildly diverse opinion as Ben Agger, Zygmunt Bauman, Barry Cooper, Terry Eagleton, Anthony Giddens, Jürgen Habermas, Ernesto Laclau, Irving Layton, C.B. Macpherson, Eli Mandel, Herbert Marcuse, W.L. Morton, J.G.A. Pocock, Charles Taylor, George Woodcock and, of course, Arthur Kroker. As academic social critics and literary theorists go, these ain't small potatoes!

Being utterly out of the *avant-garde* loop, I wasn't among the first to get the hint that there was more to Arthur Kroker than the extensive footnotes, unparsable prose, intimations of irrationalism and fuzzball concepts normally attributable to postliterate chatterers. When, however, I noticed that my newly purchased copy of the Winter, 1984 edition of the *CJPST* had abandoned its earlier dull pumpkin pulp hue (though not its ever so respectable typeface and properly restrained inside lay-out) to display "before" and "after" pictures of Elvis Presley on a shocking pink background with the caption "Cynical Commodity," I knew something was up. When I then read the front cover Baudrillardian bromide accompanying Elvis: "This time we are in a full universe, a space radiating with power but also cracked, like a shattered windshield still holding together," I finally figured it out. Arthur Kroker was a force with which to be reckoned.

And to think: Brian Mulroney had yet to sing a mock-Irish duet with Ronald Reagan.

## *Arthur Kroker and the Cage*

Now for the tough stuff: I have long admired the words that Max Weber used as he was coming to the close of *The Protestant Ethic and the Spirit of Capitalism*. As early as 1904, he had pretty much summed up the twenthieth century: "The modern economic order [and its accompanying technology would]," he declared, "determine the lives of all the individuals who are born into this mechanism . . . with irresistible force until the last ton of fossilized coal is burnt."[12] Then, in language that belied his fame as the exemplar of objective social science, Weber foresaw that life in the frenzied materialism and ruthless competition of late capitalism would be lived as in an "iron cage." His prognosis was bleak:

> No one knows who will live in this cage in the future, or whether at the end of this tremendous development entirely new prophets will arise, or there will be a great rebirth of old ideas and ideals, or, if neither, mechanized petrification, embellished with a sort of convulsive self-importance. For of the last stage of this cultural development, it might well be truly said: "Specialists without spirit, sensualists without heart; this nullity imagines that it has attained a level of civilization never before achieved."[13]

Arthur Kroker goes him one better. Arthur Kroker is not of the iron age. A century after Weber, we need worry less about the last tonne of coal than the next gram of nuclear waste. Our age is not industrial but electronic. And Arthur Kroker – possible accusations of "convulsive self-importance" or at least of clever self-promotion aside – knows better than most of us about the characteristics and dimensions of our silicon cells. "The electronic cage," he tells us, "is that point where technology comes alive, acquires organicity, and takes possession of us."[14] Neo-Luddite hyperbole at the dawn of biotechnology? Perhaps, but it is well to step back and see Kroker *in situ*, uttering his own words.

## Technology and Virtual Life

Canada's beloved George Grant, who imported the very wisest sayings of Nietzsche and the most troubling notions of Heidegger, is revered as well by Kroker, but he also dissents:

> Heidegger was wrong. Technology is not something restless, dynamic and ever expanding, but just the opposite. The will to technology equals the will to virtuality. And the will to virtuality is about the recline of western civilization: a great shutting down of experience, with a veneer of technological dynamism over an inner reality of inertia, exhaustion and disappearances.[15]

Kroker's somewhat precious microtopics ("Dead Dogs and Daddy under the Christmas Tree," "The Pleasure of Catastrophe," "Panic Penis," "Panic Plague," "Panic Politics" and "Blurred Images of Panic Bodies Moving to Escape Velocity at Warp Speeds") seem rather too contrived.

But two things should be remembered:

1. John Maynard Keynes' observation that the apparently pragmatic behaviour and comfortably banal assumptions of today's "madmen in authority" and "practical men" – CEOs and grocery clerks – merely echo the musings of some ancient "academic scribbler"[16]; although contemporary corporate communications retain few spaces for humane language, Kroker's message is, in the end, deeply humane.

2. Arthur Kroker points to the evisceration of real life. He urges us to notice how our direct experience is replaced by simulacra, by synthetic substitutions for reality. His imaginative ascriptions such as "cold sex" (Madonna mutant), "pure sex" (Michael Jackson), "dead sex" (Elvis)[17] and, perhaps, "virtual sex" (Britney Spears, for a time the iconic professional virgin with breast

implants) show a devaluing of any intimacy not initiated or mediated by machines.

Provocatively and playfully turning language back upon itself in the quest for what literary critic Kenneth Burke once called "perspective by incongruity,"[18] Kroker announces that "the computer has no memory, if by memory we mean the presence of political judgment and aesthetic reflection."[19] Everything is data in cold storage! In a particularly compelling narrative on the subject of "memory crash," Kroker explains that a major effect of digital communication is the abandonment of chronology, pattern and coherence in the assembly of information. "Recombinant" history is familiarly discussed in his book *Spasm* using the example of everyday "sampler" music recordings.[20]

## Stories

Arthur Kroker begins by acknowledging that natural human memory is selective. Vast numbers of facts are ordered according to the predilections of historians, and arranged in comprehensible themes that impute "meaning" to the jumble of recalled events. While neither complete nor objective, the stories we tell ourselves do manage to make our past intelligible. When, as always happens, competing versions of the same history appear, the resulting dialogue, debate and disputation sometimes lead to at least a temporary negotiated consensus. Few uncontested truths are told, but enough common understanding can be generated to permit us to keep living and talking together within a sustainable "discourse community." So it happens that our memories – whether public or personal – constitute a useful fiction that serves (again using a Kenneth Burke phrase) as an "equipment for living."[21] Not so with sampler music.

## Data

Decontextualized data, as in the case of digitalized sound stored in computers, can be retrieved randomly and recombined according to choices made by android processors in what Kroker calls, "transactional space." Therein, art is reconstructed outside of time, in multiple ranges quite beyond the creative intention of the composers, the attentive reflection of critics, and the authentic appreciation of an audience. "Art," he says, "is now a quantum fluctuation: a phase shift where all the old classical certainties dissolve, and where everything can finally be uncertain, probabilistic, and indeterminate."[22] We now face "a manic art of dispersion and retrieval that marks the dissolution and cancellation of the social field. A quantum art that moves into sonic over-drive, actually dissolving into a detritus of acceleration."[23] Such vertiginous prose may itself be symptomatic of the euphoria of the technological fetishism that Kroker elsewhere condemns as leading only to the revisitation of "the territory of remembered objects but remembered in a distorted way."[24] Or, it may simply and accurately mimic the noise that surrounds us.

Arthur Kroker then extends his analysis from sampler music to the more worrisome fields of sampler genetics ("Why shouldn't genes go cybernetic?"[25]), sampler politics, sampler economics and sampler strategies for environmental survival. Recombinant art may be a valid form of individual creativity, an electronically mediated collage of pictures, sounds, shapes and written words cleverly arranged to startle, amuse or instruct. The juxtaposition of incongruous material for didactic purposes nonetheless implies the willingness to test the boundaries of reason; but, when judgmental agnosticism goes further and seeks to erase those specific boundaries or to deny the legitimacy of any boundaries at all, it becomes monstrous. It allows "creation science" equal time with evolution. It permits UFOlogy the same status as astronomy. In the name of an uncritical cultural relativity, it equates cannibalism with French cuisine, no longer distinguishing between Hannibal Lecter and Julia Child. It goes far beyond Jeremy Bentham's crude utilitarian admonition that the quantity of pleasure being equal, push-pin is the equal of poetry, for it dispenses both with all empirical standards of judging facts and with any normative standards, even those that might privilege pleasure over pain.

Arthur Kroker insists that Weber's "dark intimation has already been eclipsed by our descent into the electronic cage of virtual reality. This electronic cage," he continues, "is driven by specialists fiercely possessed by the vision of technology as freedom, which can be so seductive because of the promise of a fantastic extension of the range of human (electronic) experience."[26]

## Freedom and Technology

We are especially susceptible to the attraction of information technology because we are beyond Nietzsche, who experienced an unmediated realization of the death of God. We are beyond Weber, who recoiled from the algorithm of greed in an age not yet dominated by the motor car. We (to say nothing of our children and our children's children) are "a generation born already post-historical . . . we can only understand technology as freedom because for us the language of technology – fractals, holograms, brownian motion, chaos theory, smart drugs, data uplinks – is coeval with our own identity."[27] Here, then, is the connection with conservatism and with the technologically obsolete language of George Grant.

## Deprivation

In the essay, "A Platitude," which closed *Technology and Empire*, Grant concluded:

all languages of good except the language of the drive for free-dom have disintegrated, so it is just to pass some antique wind to speak of goods that belong to man as man. Yet the answer is always the same: if we cannot so speak, then we can either only celebrate or stand in silence before that drive. Only in lis-tening for the intimations of deprivation can we live critically in that dynamo.[28]

Arthur Kroker plays us a cyberpunk cacophony of deprival. His recombinant, mutant, metamorphosed, total immersion, postmodernist, postcapitalist, postcommunist, poststructuralist, posthistorical, postcritical, pre-posthumous cant may irritate some and dazzle others (pop philosopher Mark Kingwell surely hit the mark when he suggested that "a lot of Kroker's fans don't really know what the books mean but they like them anyway"[29]). Still, Kroker descends into lucidity often enough to remind us that our culture is degenerating. When he sometimes displays what seems like a lurid interest in the cyber-fringes of body piercing and automated bank tellers, he is only lightly masking an urgent sense of loss.

"Any intimations of authentic deprival are precious," argued George Grant, "because they are the ways through which intimations of good, unthinkable in public terms, may yet appear to us."[30] Marshall McLuhan, in the alternative, understood that electronic communications technologies privileged the medium over the message, substituting new rhetorical and machine-generated special effects for com-monly shared ideas.

So two questions arise:

1. How can an awareness of deprival be launched into cyberspace?
2. Apart from blaming Protestantism for everything wicked in the world, how could McLuhan seek to infuse his Catholic sensibilities into electronic circuitry?

## The Politics of Bill Gates

In an exercise that some may choose to consider an example of compressed analogy related to the anecdotal base of the influential "New Historicism" of the 1980s, Kroker attempts to answer both questions.[31] His brief, poignant juxtaposition of events (barely coincidental as mere data but "deeply entwined" in Kroker's story) links the launching of Windows 95 and the fall of Srebenica. For him, it is the (almost?) "final settlement of human flesh in the last days of the twentieth century: the bitter division of the world into virtual flesh and surplus flesh."[32] As Bill Gates sold his new compulsory software package, the United Nations allowed the destruction of one of its "safe havens" in what has euphemistically been called the "former Yugoslavia," and lots and lots of people were wounded, maimed, mutilated and exterminated.

Arthur Kroker put it this way:

> Windows 95 opens out onto the dominant ideology and privileged life position of digital flesh. It installs the new codes of the master occupants of virtual worlds: frenzied devotion to cyber-business, life in a multi-media virtual context, digital tunnel vision, and, most of all, embedded deep in the cerebral cortex of the virtual elite an I-chip: I, that is, for complete indifference. Technological acceleration is accompanied by a big shutting-down of ethical perception.[33]

Arthur Kroker's conclusion to this short piece is worth repeating in full:

> In technology as in life, every opening is also a closing, and what is closed down by the tech hype of Windows 95 is consciousness of surplus flesh. That's Srebenica: the surplus flesh of Bosnian Muslims who do not have anything to contribute to virtual worlds: fit subjects only to be ethnically, and physically, disappeared. They can be ethnically cleansed because they have first been technically cleansed. They are surplus to world domination in a cyber-box.[34]

## Marx and Lenin and So On

Which brings up the fateful Leninist question (appropriated from Leo Tolstoy, who appropriated it from Chernyshevsky): What is to be done? What, in particular, is to be done while patiently awaiting the proletariat's long promised assumption of its revolutionary historical role? Considerable forbearance will surely be required; after all, preliminary steps must include the dissociation of the masses from professional sports franchises as the loci of their deep political loyalty and from seeing *The $64,000 Question* or the inflated *Who Wants to Be a Millionaire?* as simulacra of overcoming the gap between poverty and wealth. Much thought must also be given to revolutionary intellectual work since the grand theories of social life and social change "are all dimly perceived through slogans." As Harvard geneticist emeritus Richard Lewontin reminds us: "Survival of the fittest, like penis envy, is the opiate of the masses."[35]

The complete project before us can be daunting. Michael A. Weinstein – collaborator and contributor to Arthur and Marilouise Kroker's erudite anthology *Power and Ideology in the Age of Lenin in Ruins* – has, for example, no trouble berating the "parasite-predators" of corporate late capitalism.[36] He scolds Ronald Reagan for his "postmodern mind . . . at the level of the paneled basement den."[37] He rails against the apocalyptic vision "of the day in which Jacobinism and capitalism finally fuse into techno-fascism."[38] Criticism, however, is easy. It can be jocose, inspirational and profound (though rarely all three). So, if there were any members of the Business Council on National Issues or inmates of the Fraser Institute with the wit to penetrate their earnest ideological fog and see their own casuistries for the cruel jokes they are, such critiques could be devastating.

On the other hand, articulating cogent alternatives to neoliberal sophistry and formulating sensible methods to achieve practical political goods can discourage equally the subtlest and the shrillest left-wing derogators as they grapple with the enduring problem that faces radical theorists and activists. How are they to blast away the opacity of listless working class heroes supine and somnolent on couches in their suburban caves, contemplating dancing shadows, occasionally clicking their remote control devices and false consciously exercising the power of consumer choice? How are they to communicate a theory of power that does not lead inexorably to hopelessness? The questions are barely rhetorical.

And yet – and yet, there is hope. Part of the hope involves dispensing with the epistemologically obdurate Platonism that has long dominated much of Western thought in general and, unhappily and unnecessarily, leftist thought in particular. This part requires the recognition of random or merely quirky empirical variations not as annoying anomalies that mess up perfectly formed theories, but as indispensable elements of social change itself. Another part implies the acceptance of subversive artistry as a necessary form of political action that can assist the process of deconstructing the very language of power, and publicly demonstrate how vulnerable even fearfully entrenched power can be.[39]

Arthur Kroker understands what power is. When he and Weinstein elaborated their theory of the virtual class, they were not jettisoning orthodox Marxism in favour of an amorphous caviling of lifestyle, a *pousse-cafe* analysis of socioeconomic class divisions. Instead, they were affirming the importance of ideology for the maintenance of social control. They were calling attention to the importance of managing the media and the messages of electronic information for those seeking ideological hegemony. They were thereby emphasizing the primacy of free speech, the highest value of the Diogenes the Cynic and the bane of cynical manipulators of power everywhere.

For the present, messages seem to flow freely enough.[40] People throughout China knew of the 1989 slaughter in Tiananmen Square because no government could stop faxes from North America. By similar means, people in southern Ontario and British Columbia quickly learned the grisly details revealed at the Karla Homolka and Robert William Pickton murder trials despite judicial "gag orders" simply by downloading information freely published and posted on U.S. media web sites. Electronic information respects neither physical space nor political borders, nor certainly juridical injunctions. The virtual world knew early on about President Bill, Monica Lewinsky and the deliberations of the Starr Chamber; it also knew about the murder of the royal family in Katmandu within minutes of the event, an event kept for some time from the people of Nepal. Just as the penny post permitted the unprecedented coordination of Chartist action in the mid-nineteenth century, the Internet now seems the organizing instrument of choice for worldwide demonstrations against globalization.[41] In all of this, Arthur Kroker occasionally and perhaps whimsically takes heart. He presents himself as a recombinant techno-populist nodding approvingly toward attempts to wire whole cities for electronic town meetings and digital plebiscites. Arthur Kroker's hopes may not be entirely empty.

Over thirty years ago Martin Nicolaus, then an aspirant academic with an "in-your-face" attitude, addressed the Annual Meeting of the American Sociological Association in Boston. He accused mainstream sociology of "servility." He insisted that the practice of sociology was a "criminal activity" and that sociologists were double agents, winning the trust of the dispossessed, and then collecting information to be turned over to their class enemies. "So far," he observed, "sociologists have been schlepping this knowledge along a one-way chain, taking knowledge from the people, giving knowledge to the rulers. What if," Nicolaus then asked, "that machinery were reversed? What if the habits, problems, secrets and unconscious motivations of the wealthy were daily scrutinized by a thousand systematic researchers, were hourly pried into, analyzed and cross-referenced, tabulated and published in a hundred inexpensive mass circulation journals and written so that even a fifteen-year-old high school drop-out could understand it and predict the actions of his landlord, manipulate, and control him?"[42] The question is no longer entirely hypothetical, though the postulate of mass circulation journals in "hard copy" may be a trifle anachronous. One example is <www.rabble.ca>, a web site launched on 18 April, 2001. This on-line newspaper is published by activist Judy Rebick, and edited by ex-CBC journalist Judy MacDonald. With links to the Canadian Centre for Policy Alternatives, the Council of Canadians, the Canadian Centre for Social Justice and many other like-minded organizations, it has potential. Says columnist Michelle Landsberg: "I'm daring to hope that Rabble.ca will be what I've longed for, the medium that has the depth and the reach to inform, gather and galvanize us to save our country from total corporate ruination."[43]

Arthur Kroker also knows that the medium isn't the whole message, and that control over information technology means control over information in an age when the means of communication are more invasive than ever before. The obvious implication is that aspirant policy innovators, who seek to involve citizens in a participatory process leading to political outcomes that genuinely reflect the "will of the people," have two related challenges. One is to ensure access to electronic information exchange for, at the very least, everyone affected by particular policy choices. The other is to minimize the ability of established interests to dominate electronic discussion both by controlling who has access to the technology of information dissemination, and by deciding what government or corporate information shall be classified as exempt from public scrutiny. What seem inevitable are calls for a "bill of information rights" to include, perhaps, guarantees of privacy for individuals now threatened by public and private cyber-surveillance, and obligations of public disclosure for corporate and government institutions.

Laudable as such initiatives might be, I worry some. Working men once thought that universal male franchise would win them a world. Women once thought that female suffrage would win them at least half a world. Somehow, though, the ideas of John Stuart Mill and Harriet Taylor Mill concerning both the legitimacy of democracy and the need for a knowledgeable electorate must be re-addressed in the context of emerging communications technology.

Optimists will agree with the pronouncements of "media comprehensivist" Frank Zingrone who, with assistance from Ilya Prigogine and Isabelle Stengers, tells us:

> A single individual with a brilliant idea and an attractive web site can start a billion-dollar business. Borrowing from Thomas Jefferson, one person with a network is a majority. The small fluctuations of one person's articulate dissent, added by media to a stressed disequilibrium, can become amplified into gigantic, structure-breaking waves.[44]

At the same time, Zingrone renders a tame version of the negative side thus: "Complex media controls [seek] to effectively manage human consciousness everywhere as if it were an advertising demographic. The gatekeepers of this control activity are very large transnational corporations." And, as for articulate dissenters, "attempts by governments to control the Net are unrelenting."[45]

Cyber-populism may soon allow us to experience authoritative digital plebiscites on the questions of which dispossessed group most deserves to be cut off social assistance, who among the poor should have their lifestyle criminalized, which public services might most profitably be privatized, to which level of an inevitably lower standard of living we must sink in the interest of greater corporate profitability in the global marketplace, and which terrorist training camp to target. Since the agenda can easily be set by neoliberal authorities, the answers to loaded multiple choice questions defeat the purpose of expressing the popular will. (Ask any professional pollster!) So, before the plausibility of an informed citizenry has been totally "dumbed" out of existence, it is required of us that we reflect deeply on the notion of the civic society, a polity wherein concern for the public good takes at least an equal place with concern for private interest.

If we do not do this or if our reflections produce no pertinent political results, corporate domination of cyberspace will oblige perhaps the most potentially liberating technology since the printing press to succumb to the dictates of a cultural, economic and political agenda that will be anything but democratic. The stakes, moreover, have seldom been higher. As Tom Hayden, the former 1960s radical and California State Senator says:

> [Citizens are now] confronting the very nature of the way economics, environmentalism and human rights are going to be shaped for the rest of our lives. The so-called new world order has to do with everything: exports, prevailing wages, sweatshops, sea turtles, the price and quality of food. The Vietnam War was going to end . . . but the new world order will not.[46]

Standing aside, with the understated good sense of a dispassionate Canadian observer, Arthur Kroker concludes: "We live now with the great secret, and the equally great anxiety, that the technological experience is both Orwellian and hopelessly utopian – the smell of exterminism [is] in the air."[47]

## An Arthur Kroker Sampler

Arthur Kroker, *Technology and the Canadian Mind: Innis / McLuhan / Grant* (Montreal: New World Perspectives, 1984).

Arthur Kroker and Marilouise Kroker, *Body Invaders: Panic Sex in America* (Montreal: New World Perspectives, 1987).

Arthur Kroker, "Panic Value: Bacon, Colville, Baudrillard and the Aesthetics of Deprivation," in John Fekete, ed., *Life After Postmodernism: Essays on Value and Culture* (New York: St. Martin's Press, 1987).

Arthur Kroker and Marilouise Kroker, eds., *The Hysterical Male: New Feminist Theory* (Montreal: New World Perspectives, 1987).

Arthur Kroker, Marilouise Kroker and David Cook, *Panic Encyclopedia* (Montreal: New World Perspectives, 1989).

Arthur Kroker and Marilouise Kroker, eds., *Ideology and Power in the Age of Lenin in Ruins* (Montreal: New World Perspectives, 1991).

Arthur Kroker, *The Possessed Individual: Technology and the French Postmodern* (Montreal: New World Perspectives, 1991).

Arthur Kroker and Marilouise Kroker, eds., *The Last Sex: Feminism and Outlaw Bodies* (Montreal: New World Perspectives, 1993).

Arthur Kroker, *Spasm: Virtual Reality, Android Music and Electric Flesh* (Montreal: New World Perspectives, 1993).

Arthur Kroker and Michael A. Weinstein, *Data Trash: The Theory of the Virtual Class* (Montreal: New World Perspectives, 1995).

Arthur Kroker, *Hacking the Future: Stories for the Flesh-Eating 90s* (Montreal: New World Perspectives, 1996).

Arthur Kroker and Marilouise Kroker, eds., *Digital Delirium* (Montreal: New World Perspectives, 1997).

Arthur Kroker and Marilouise Kroker, eds., <ctheory.net>

## Notes

This is a revision of a paper presented at the Twentieth Annual Meeting of the American Culture Association in Orlando, Florida (April, 1998). An earlier version was published in *The Innovation Journal* (September 3, 1999), portions of which are reproduced here with permission.

1. This is not to say that some performers did not see the wisdom of moving north. Examples include *Mr. Rogers'* alumnus Ernie "*Mr. Dressup*" Coombs (who stayed in Canada after Fred Rogers left the CBC for PBS, and who died shortly after the last broad-

cast of *Mr. Rogers' Neighbourhood* and seven days after the destruction of the World Trade Center), rocker Ronnie Hawkins, country singer Jesse Winchester, *Homicide: Life on the Street*'s Yaphet Kotto and *Law and Order*'s Michael Moriarty. It does not deny that celebrated novelist-cum-screen-writer John Irving does not spend his summers on an island in Georgian Bay as does author Calvin Trillin in Nova Scotia. It also allows that many Canadians who gained fame and fortune in New York or Los Angeles have returned (some of their own free will).

2. It is reliably reported that one wag commented: "I knew he couldn't have said that in Canada. He didn't call him 'Mr.' Watson and he didn't say 'please.'"

3. Jack Granatstein, "The 100 Most Important Canadians in History," *Maclean's* (1 July, 1998).

4. William Burrill, "Canucks who count," *eye* (8 July, 1998). Though critical of Burrill, I cannot fault his judgement that Granatstein erred in calling Vincent Massey the greatest Canadian of all time.

5. H. A. Innis, *The Strategy of Culture* (Toronto: University of Toronto Press, 1952), p. 16.

6. Quoted in John Robert Colombo, ed., *Colombo's Canadian Quotations* (Edmonton: Hurtig, 1974), p. 208.

7. *Ibid.*

8. George Grant, *Lament for a Nation: The Defeat of Canadian Nationalism* (Toronto: McClelland and Stewart, 1965), p. 68.

9. Arthur Kroker and Michael A. Weinstein, *Data Trash: The Theory of the Virtual Class* (Montréal: New World Perspectives, 1995), p. 158.

10. John Leonard, *When the Kissing Had to Stop* (New York: New Press, 1999), p. 154. Leonard's only explicit reservation is that Kroker too easily "buys into AI machine dreams against all evidence that the genetic engineers are lots farther along, custom-combining organic mutants, than the cyberneticists [who are nowhere] near an artificial hand or eye, much less consciousness." *Ibid.*

11. Mark Kingwell, "Geek with an Argument," *Saturday Night* (February, 1996), pp. 75-77.

12. Max Weber, *The Protestant Ethic and the Spirit of Capitalism* (New York: Charles Scribner's Sons, 1958), p. 181.

13. *Ibid.*, p. 182.

14. Arthur Kroker, *Spasm: Virtual Reality, Android Music and Electric Flesh* (Montréal: New World Perspectives, 1993), p. 7.

15. *Ibid.*

16. John Maynard Keynes, *The General Theory of Employment, Interest and Money* (London: Macmillan, 1936), p. 383.

17. Kroker, *op. cit.*, p. 19.

18. Kenneth Burke, *Attitudes Toward History* (Boston: Beacon, 1961), pp. 308-314.

19. Kroker, *op. cit.*, p. 31.

20. *Ibid.*, pp. 32-33.

21. Kenneth Burke, *The Philosophy of Literary Form* (New York: Vintage, 1957), pp. 253-262.

22. Kroker, *op. cit.*, p. 33.

23. *Ibid.*

24. *Ibid.*, p. 32.

25. *Ibid.*, p. 38.

26. *Ibid.*, p. 37.

27. *Ibid.*

28. George Grant, *Technology and Empire: Perspectives on North America* (Toronto: Anansi, 1969), p. 141.

29. Kingwell, *op. cit.*, p. 75.

30. George Grant, *loc. cit.*

31. See Catharine Gallagher and Stephen Greenblatt, *Practicing New Historicism* (Chicago: University of Chicago Press, 2000). His method also bears comparison to anthropologist Clifford Geertz's concept of "transactional *praxis*" nicely explicated in "In Search of North Africa," *The New York Review* (22 April, 1971), pp. 22-24 and his technique of "thick description" exemplified in his account of the Balinese cockfight in *The Interpretation of Cultures* (New York: Basic Books, 1973), pp. 403-404.

32. Arthur Kroker and Marilouise Kroker, *Hacking the Future: Stories for the Flesh-Eating 90s* (Montréal: New World Perspectives, 1996), p. 36.

33. *Ibid.*

34. *Ibid.*

35. Richard Lewontin, *It Ain't Necessarily So: The Dream of the Human Genome Project and Other Illusions* (New York: New York Review Books, 2000), p. 65.

36. Michael A. Weinstein, "The Dark Night of the Liberal Spirit and the Dawn of the Savage," in Arthur Kroker and Marilouise Kroker, eds., *Ideology and Power in the Age of Lenin in Ruins* (Montréal: New World Perspectives, 1991), p. 219.

37. *Ibid.*, p. 221.

38. *Ibid.*, p. 224.

39. Wonderful insights and suggestions can be found in the neglected work of Henry S. Kariel. See, for example, *Saving Appearances:*

*The Reestablishment of Political* Science (Belmont: Duxbury Press, 1972), *Beyond Liberalism, Where Relations Grow* (San Francisco: Chandler & Sharp, 1977), and *The Desperate Politics of Postmodernism* (Amherst, University of Massachusetts Press, 1989).

40. "Enough" is, of course, a relative term. During the past decade, customs officers have confiscated gay magazines and medical textbooks entering Canada, computer bulletin board services have begun practicing self-censorship fearing criminal obscenity charges, Tipper Gore did the best she could with music lyrics and Christians burned CDs by Bruce Springsteen, Disney videos such as *Pinocchio* and books by Judy Blume and J. K. Rowling. That they are satisfied with burning books when they used to burn people may be viewed as a token of progress.

41. If, as some have warned, the authorities have equal access to rebellious web sites, it is of no tactical consequence. Anti-globalization demonstrations, unlike the followers of Osama bin Laden, are about publicity not conspiracy. Marx and Engels proudly boasted: "The Communists disdain to conceal their views and aims" (Karl Marx and Friedrich Engels, *The Communist Manifesto* (New York: Appleton-Century-Crofts, 1955), p. 46. If it was good enough for them, it is certainly good enough for Avi Lewis and Naomi Klein.

42. Martin Nicolaus, "Remarks at the ASA Convention," mimeo (Boston, 1968), pp. 2-3.

43. Michelle Landsberg, "Rabble.ca may rouse us from our torpor," *The Toronto Star* (14 April, 2001), p. M-1. In return, I dare to hope that Ms. Landsberg now has second thoughts about what her close associates truly accomplished – also about thirty years ago – when they purged the "Waffle" from the Ontario NDP.

44. Frank Zingrone, *The Media Symplex* (Toronto: Stoddart, 2001), p. 21. See also Ilya Prigogine and Isabelle Stengers, *Order Out of Chaos: Man's New Dialogue with Nature* (New York: Bantam, 1984).

45. *Ibid.*

46. Quoted in Mary Gordon, "Out of Order," *Campus.ca* (February, 2001), p. 13.

47. Arthur Kroker, Marilouise Kroker and David Cook, *Panic Encyclopedia* (Montréal: New World Perspectives, 1989), p. 73. As, yet again, the world changes forever, "exterminism," seems temporarily to have the upper hand. See Dion Dennis, "The World Trade Center and the Rise of the Security State," *CTHEORY: Theory, Technology and Culture*, (Event-scene 98) Vol. 24, 3 (18 September, 2001)

# Contributors

Douglas Bailie is a doctoral candidate in the Department of History and Classics at the University of Alberta in Edmonton, Alberta. His dissertation is on the rise of the theatre industry in Canada.

Howard A. Doughty has been with Seneca College since 1969. He currently teaches Cultural Anthropology and Philosophy in the Faculty of Applied Arts and Health Sciences at its campus in King City, Ontario, and is a shop steward for the Ontario Public Service Employees Union, Local 560. Formerly editor of *Bridges: Explorations in Science, Technology and Society* (1986-1991) and *The College Quarterly* (1992-1997), he has been Book Review Editor of *The Innovation Journal* since 1998.

Susan Ellis is a lawyer and a doctoral candidate in the Department of English at the University of British Columbia in Vancouver. She has published work on Michael Ondaatje as well as a number of reviews in *Canadian Literature*. Her main interests include contemporary Canadian writing, oral poetry, and topics in law and literature. She is also involved in the Canadian Law and Society Association.

Brian L. Flack has published two novels, *In Seed Time* and *With A Sudden and Terrible Clarity*, has written two more and is at work on yet another, has scattered poems here and there, some published in Canadian literary magazines as well as a book, *I Side Up*, and has edited twelve anthologies of short fiction produced by the members of a Seneca College Creative Writing Seminar he created and has been leading for seventeen years.

Gordon Hatt was born in Wiarton, Ontario in 1957. He attended York University in Toronto as a studio major. He received his Honours B.A and M.A. in Art History from the University of Toronto. He has been curator at Cambridge Galleries since 1997.

Diane E. Meaghan is Visiting Scholar at the Ontario Institute for Studies in Education in Toronto. She has a Ph.D. in Sociology from the University of Toronto. A professional psychological counselor early in her career, she has taught Sociology and Women's Studies at the postsecondary level for the past twenty-eight years. She is currently conducting research on international sex work.

Ches Skinner is Dean of the Faculty of Fine Arts at the University of Lethbridge, Alberta. His continuing interest in Canadian theatre and performance art was most recently demonstrated at the 32nd annual meeting of the Popular Culture Association in Toronto (March, 2002) in a paper entitled "Lunatics, Lovers, and Poets: Louis Nowri's Cosi."

Michael R. Welton is a professor of adult education at Mount St. Vincent University, Halifax, Nova Scotia. He writes about adult education history and critical theoretical approaches to adult learning. His earlier work includes *In Defense of the Lifeworld* (Albany: SUNY Press, 1995), and his latest book is *Little Mosie from the Margaree: a Biography of Moses Michael Coady* (Toronto: Thompson Books, 2001).

Printed in March 2007
at Gauvin Press, Gatineau, Québec